"Readers of this book should prepare to be surprised and to have their presuppositions shaken. Kelly, clearly a good teacher, leads us through the Bible's gradual development of an understanding of the figure of Satan from Genesis to Revelation, as well as the interpretations of early Christian writers. His conclusions are challenging but very important for believers. An added bonus is the clarification of the book of Revelation, what it says and what it doesn't. For that alone, the book is worth reading."

—Irene Nowell, OSB
Mount St. Scholastica
Adjunct professor
Saint John's School of Theology

"Joseph F. Kelly has written an excellent study on the role of Satan in the Jewish and Christian traditions. Satan is a multifold character with complicated lineage, and this book brings many sources together to produce a thorough synthetic analysis. Kelly examines biblical sources, Jewish and Christian commentary, rabbinic and patristic texts, and contemporary theological discourse on Satan and the problem of evil. Kelly's book will be of interest to scholars and students interested in this topic."

—Jeanne-Nicole Saint-Laurent
Assistant Professor of Theology
Marquette University

D1047682

Who Is Satan?
According to the Scriptures

Joseph F. Kelly

LITURGICAL PRESS
Collegeville, Minnesota

www.litpress.org

Nihil Obstat: Reverend Robert Harren, *Censor deputatus.*

Imprimatur: ✛ Most Reverend John F. Kinney, J.C.D., D.D., Bishop of Saint Cloud, Minnesota, June 10, 2013.

Cover design by Jodi Hendrickson. Cover image: Thinkstock.

1   2   3   4   5   6   7   8   9

Library of Congress Cataloging-in-Publication Data

Kelly, Joseph F. (Joseph Francis), 1945–
    Who is Satan? according to the scriptures / Joseph F. Kelly.
        pages cm
    Includes bibliographical references.
    ISBN 978-0-8146-3516-2 — ISBN 978-0-8146-3541-4 (e-book)
    1. Devil—Biblical teaching.   I. Title.

    BS680.D56K46   2013
    235'.47—dc23   2013014300

To my children-in-law:
Jung-A Kelly, Bradley Klein, and Robert Wagoner

Contents

Preface

During more than four decades of teaching religion, I have encountered many questions about Satan, especially when my courses deal with the problem of evil. The students generally want their beliefs to harmonize with those of the Bible and their churches. They wonder what the Bible says about the devil and also belief *itself* in the devil when psychology and other modern scientific disciplines seemed to have driven him into the realm of myth. They are also confused about a number of issues, such as the following: Why does 666 signify the devil? Is Satan the Antichrist, or does that term mean a human?

These are legitimate questions because many popular writers and filmmakers have mashed a number of diverse traditions into a semi-comprehensible whole, even though what they usually do is distort Christian teaching and tradition about Satan.

This little book will certainly not stop someone else from writing something titled *Satan and His Brother Antichrist* or, in a less patriarchal vein, *Is the Antichrist a Woman?* What this book will do is introduce the reader to what the Bible actually says about Satan and other evil biblical figures.

Why just the Bible? Because the Christian satanic tradition is immense. America's foremost scholar of

Satan, Jeffrey Burton Russell, needed four volumes to explicate it. Treating Satan in the Bible will make this book more accessible to those not able to delve into twenty centuries of traditions and theology about Satan.

There is another reason for focusing on Scripture. Liturgical Press has a strong Roman Catholic orientation, but it is an ecumenical publisher, and this book is by an ecumenical Roman Catholic. Christian churches agree and disagree, fraternally, on any number of issues, but all accept the authority of Scripture. I hope to make this book more ecumenical by treating the one source all churches accept as authoritative.

Many people helped to make this book possible. First and foremost is Hans Christoffersen, publisher, academic and trade division, at Liturgical Press, who was open to the idea of an introductory book on Satan and who has provided support and encouragement throughout.

Several people at John Carroll University likewise provided support. I received a reduced teaching load to write this book, and my thanks to my (then) chairperson, Dr. John Spencer, for recommending me for the reduced load. My thanks also to the dean of the College of Arts and Sciences, Dr. Jeanne Colleran, who supported my request, and Dr. John Day, academic vice president, who formally awarded me the load reduction.

To carry out the necessary work, I needed specific resources. My thanks to Dr. Lauren Bowen, associate academic vice president and chair of the University Committee on Research and Service, who granted me funds to purchase needed materials.

Helping me with my initial work on Satan in the New Testament was Jureell Sison, my graduate assistant in 2011–12; my thanks to him for his fine work. Helping me with the later work and doing a great deal of proofreading was my current graduate assistant Kristen

Pungitore. She did thorough work, did it quickly, and was never hesitant to suggest some helpful alterations to the text. I am grateful to her for making this a better book.

Any deficiencies in the book are the sole responsibility of the author.

This book is dedicated to my three children-in-law: Jung-A Kelly, wife of my son Robert and mother of my granddaughter Marion Yena Kelly; Bradley Klein, husband of my daughter Alicia; and Robert Wagoner, husband of my daughter Amy and father of my granddaughters Hannah Laine and Jenna Grace Wagoner.

As always, my deepest gratitude goes to my wife, Ellen Marie Kelly, a loving partner of forty-five years who has always encouraged my work and made sacrifices so that I could write. No words could ever say what she means to me or what I owe to her.

Joseph F. Kelly
John Carroll University

CHAPTER ONE

The Problem of Satan

In his *Christian Doctrine for Everyman: An Introduction to Baptist Beliefs*, Jimmy Millikin says, "We know they [demons] are real personalities. They are capable of intelligent, voluntary actions. . . . We know also that they are spiritual beings . . . with great power. Demons are 'unclean spirits,' which means they are depraved and wicked in their nature. . . . The work of demons is essentially the same as that of Satan. Their main occupation is . . . opposing the will and purposes of God" (134).

Davis Britton in his *Historical Dictionary of Mormonism* says Satan is a "real spirit personage who leads the forces of evil and tries to defeat God's purpose. In the pre-mortal existence this spirit, also a child of God, rebelled and took with him a portion of the host of Heaven. . . . Since then Satan has tried to frustrate the Plan of Salvation" (214).

The web site catholic.com says that the "Catholic Church has always held that the devil is real, not a mythical personification of evil." The site then quotes a 1975 Vatican document, *Christian Faith and Demonology*: "It is a departure from the picture painted by the Bible and Church teaching to refuse to acknowledge the devil's existence."

1

The fundamentalist web site christcenteredmall.com teaches that "Satan and his cohorts have lied, sinned, murdered, persecuted, and made war against God's creation since the Garden of Eden," and "one of the reasons the devil exists is so the children of God can grow up into the full stature of Jesus Christ."

Clearly the people behind these statements believe in the devil and take him very seriously. Yet in heavily Catholic northern New Jersey, the local professional hockey team is named the Devils. In conservative-Protestant North Carolina, college sports fans can root for the Duke University Blue Devils and the Wake Forest University Demon Deacons. In very conservative-Protestant Mississippi, fans can root for the Mississippi Valley State University women's athletic teams, which are called the Devilettes! This lack of concern about taking Satan lightly extends beyond the range of sports. Consider the San Antonio, Texas, firm, Lucifer Lighting Company. If you need heat as well as light, you can call Lucifer Furnaces, Inc., of Warrington, Pennsylvania. You can even eat demonically because the Food Network can teach you how to make Satanic Fudge Brownies.

What is going on here? How can people believe that the devil is a thoroughly evil being, roaming about the world seeking the destruction of souls, and simultaneously believe there is nothing wrong with naming athletic teams and business companies after him? Would people name teams or companies after people or groups that they truly loathe and fear? Can anyone seriously picture a team named the Tacoma Terrorists or a food company named Nazi Nachos?

Clearly, modern people, including modern believers, have conflicting views of the devil. Part of that derives from a lack of knowledge about what the church teaches about the devil and, more fundamentally, what the Bible says about him. For example, on June 6, 2006 (the sixth

day of the sixth month of the sixth year—666), news-
papers, television stations, and the web carried stories
about people who feared a day numbered 666 since that
was the number of the devil. In fact, it is not. The number 666 appears in only one place in the Bible, Revelation
13:18, and that verse says, "it is the number of a human
being, the number 666." But Christian tradition teaches
that the devil is a spiritual being, a fallen angel, and since
666 refers to a man, it simply cannot apply to Satan.

Such confusion is not unusual. The Bible has the
distinction of being the one book people do not read but
are still convinced they know what is in it. Some widely
known and often quoted "Bible" verses simply do not
exist. For example, a famous image of a peaceable kingdom is one in which, the Bible supposedly says, "the
lion will lie down with the lamb." This famous verse,
Isaiah 11:6, actually reads, "The wolf shall live with
the lamb, the leopard shall lie down with the kid, and
the calf and the lion shall browse together, and a little
child will lead them." Over centuries of misquoting, this
verse metamorphosed into the now-familiar one.

Along those same lines, many people believe that the
Gospel of Matthew tells us that three kings named
Caspar, Melchior, and Balthasar rode on camels to give
gifts to the infant Jesus. Actually all the gospel says is
that "magi" came from the East. The gospel never gives
their names, calls them kings, says they rode on camels,
or even mentions how many of them there were.

In this book our focus will be to specify, examine,
and sometimes clarify biblical teaching about the devil,
since the scriptural teachings are the essential ones that
all churches refer to. Then we will take a brief look at
postbiblical developments that magnified the devil's
role in Christianity—often leaving Scripture behind in
the process—and we will finish with a consideration of
modern attitudes and teachings about Satan.

But before we start, let us deal with several important preliminary matters.

"Satan" or "Devil"?

Who exactly are we talking about in this book?

In the Hebrew Bible (the Christian Old Testament) we find the word *satan*, meaning "adversary," a word sometimes used to refer to human beings. For example, when the sons of a man named Zeruiah challenge King David, he asks them what right they have to play the *satan* against him (2 Sam 19:22). Gradually the word *satan* was transformed to spiritual beings and then to evil spiritual beings. Eventually it came to stand for just one being, a particularly powerful one.

When this word was translated by ancient Jews into Greek—the language of the New Testament—it was rendered *diábolos*, the Greek word for "adversary." From there it became *diabolus* in Latin, which became *diavolo* in Italian, *diablo* in Spanish, *diable* in French, *Teufel* in German, and *devil* in English. Thus Satan and devil are equivalent terms. Later in the book we will see where other names such as Lucifer and Beelzebub came from.

Modern Biblical Study

Since we are focusing upon what the Bible says about the devil, we need to know something about modern biblical study or, to use the technical term, exegesis.

Biblical exegesis has become very controversial today, largely because a sizeable group of very conservative Christians, generally called fundamentalists, practice a literal understanding of much of the Bible. Their strongest focus has fallen upon the opening chapters of the book of Genesis, those dealing with the creation, the Garden of Eden, the Fall, and Noah's Flood, all of which they take as actual historical events. Since most high schools and all accredited colleges and universities teach about biological evolution and billions of years of existence for the universe, many fundamentalists have objected to what their children are learning in school, believing that modern science challenges and even mocks the Bible. Fundamentalist groups have lobbied for the teaching of creationism or intelligent design in schools, and they have established their own biblical institutes and other intellectual centers such as the Creation Museum in Petersborough, Kentucky (founded in 2007).

Let me say, with all goodwill, that I admire the faith of the fundamentalists and their great ardor to protect the Bible from what they perceive to be malicious attacks upon its veracity. But I am a Roman Catholic, and in this book we will take the approach to the Bible used by Catholic, Jewish, and mainline Protestant scholars. Obviously members of these traditions do not always agree with one another's interpretations of the Bible, but they also disagree among themselves. It is not uncommon for a Catholic scholar to propose a certain interpretation of a biblical passage, only to find another Catholic scholar disagreeing while a Jewish scholar agrees with the former and a Protestant scholar disagrees with them both. This is modern exegesis!

While modern scholars may disagree with one another about particular biblical verses, they do not disagree on the overall method of understanding the Bible. Founded mostly by the German Protestants in the nineteenth century, modern exegesis seeks to understand the world in which the Bible was written on the logical grounds that if we do not understand the place, time, environment, and worldview of the biblical writers as well as the literary genres they employed, we will never understand the biblical text.

At first glance, this does not seem to present problems, not even to fundamentalists. For example, the

Bible speaks constantly about slavery. God gave Abraham slaves. Hebrew legal codes in the books of Exodus and Leviticus take slavery for granted. Israelite monarchs owned slaves. The apostle Paul not only accepted slavery as an institution but actually told slaves who had converted to Christianity not to be concerned about being slaves (1 Cor 7:21), while the author of the First Epistle of Peter told slaves to be subject to their masters with reverence, even if the masters were abusive (1 Pet 2:18).

All modern believers must accept that most ancient Jews and Christians saw nothing wrong with slavery and accepted it as part of social and economic life. Yet what modern believer would claim that these passages justify slavery today (as nineteenth-century supporters of slavery in the United States did)?

But the important point that fundamentalists and mainline believers recognize is that this ancient practice, validated throughout the Bible, was an *ancient attitude not binding on contemporary believers*. Fundamentalists would denounce and repudiate anyone who claimed that the Bible justifies slavery for modern believers.

Mainline exegetes would agree, but they would go further. They would study how the ancient economy worked. They would point out that everyone who wrote in favor of slavery, or at least who did not condemn it, was not a slave himself (all the authors were male). Modern scholars would note how slaves were often prisoners of war or descendants of them; they would also note that men did most of the purchasing of slaves and that female slaves were often bought for sexual purposes. They would also point out that the slaves were considered property—rather like animals—and thus the owners could demand that slaves do whatever they wished. Grasping facts like these enables exegetes to understand why biblical writers could support and even defend slavery.

But modern scholars apply this same method to all of the Bible in order to understand what the biblical writers meant, because if modern believers do not know what the Bible *meant*, they cannot understand what it *means* to them.

And this is where modern scholarship parts company not just with fundamentalists but sometimes with many believers. Let me give some examples.

At the end of his gospel (24:51) and the opening of his second book, the Acts of the Apostles (1:9-10), the evangelist Luke recounts the ascension of Jesus into heaven when Jesus literally rose up into the air and disappeared into a cloud. In thousands of churches, this scene has been reproduced in stained glass, paintings, and statues.

But, modern scholars ask, how could this have happened? Luke tells us that Jesus entered heaven by going up into the air. But how can heaven be above the clouds when science has demonstrated that beyond our earth is almost all empty space with the occasional star? Modern scholars—and even a conservative theologian like Pope John Paul II—teach that heaven is a state of being, not a physical place above the sky.

So modern biblical study negates the ascension? Not at all.

Modern scholars would point out that Luke had a theological point to make. Jesus had finished his mission on earth and would now return to his Father so that the Holy Spirit could come to earth to continue Jesus' work. But in Luke's day, people believed heaven to be above the earth, a view that persisted until the scientific revolution of the sixteenth and seventeenth centuries. What modern believers must do is accept that Luke was a man of his age and that the views of his age should not be imposed on us. We can accept Luke's point that Jesus returned to his Father in heaven; we cannot accept his supposition that heaven is a place above the clouds.

This is a good example of how modern scholarship works: trying to understand what the biblical writer wrote *and why*, interpreting the biblical passage for the modern world, and demonstrating that this modern approach does not corrupt the Bible but in fact saves it.

Saves it by denying it happened physically? Yes. If moderns are told that they must accept that heaven is a place above the clouds because twenty centuries ago in a prescientific age Luke said that it was, their response will not be belief but skepticism and ultimately rejection. Biblical truth need not be literal truth.

If we can sum up the different approaches in one sentence, it would be: *Modern exegetes are willing to let the biblical writers be who they actually were while others want to force the Bible into the modern world.*

To return to the scriptural text, since Luke's account of the ascension reflects his view of the cosmos, are there other areas in which modern scholars doubt the literalness of a biblical account? Absolutely.

Modern believers want to state their religious beliefs in highly intellectual theological propositions and, where possible, back them up with facts. Ancient believers certainly did that, but they were also willing to express their beliefs in legends and even myths. Consider the account of the Exodus.

Exodus (7:14–12:30) tells us that God inflicted ten plagues upon the Egyptians because Pharaoh would not let the Hebrew slaves leave. If taken literally, we are supposed to believe that Pharaoh's stubbornness literally wrecked Egypt and harmed its people—but there was no revolution or at least a palace coup? Everyone in Egypt stood docilely by while Pharaoh did nothing to stop the destruction?

There is also a strong moral argument—the tenth plague. God is angry with Pharaoh, but instead of afflicting him with leprosy or blinding him until he relents, God murders several hundred thousand innocent Egyptian children. Does anyone today really believe in God the mass murderer? No, but you must if you take this account as a historical one.

The problem with taking so much of the Bible as absolutely factual ranges even into its very wording. Luke (11:2-4) and Matthew (6:9-14) have different versions of the Lord's Prayer, Matthew's being the familiar one. They also have different versions of the Beatitudes (Luke 6:20-23 and Matt 5:3-9), and again, Matthew's is the familiar one. It is difficult to say that we have pure historical accounts when Jesus' very words differ in the gospels.

But even this is not a problem for modern exegesis because we know that in the ancient world, much was passed along orally. Abraham lived around 1800 BC, but accounts of him, his sons, the twelve tribes, the Exodus, and so much more of early Israelite history were not written down until literally hundreds of years later. The people passed the accounts along orally, and no doubt the occasional word or phrase became lost or modified, so that the writers of the Bible would sometimes have to re-create what happened and what was said. Furthermore, what might have been important in 1500 BC may not have meant much to people living in 500 BC, and so the biblical writers worked with the accounts to make them clear to their contemporary audiences and occasionally to add material for purposes of comprehension and interpretation. We must never forget that every author writes for an audience.

This brief description of modern exegesis and of the difficulty of taking some biblical passages as factual accounts hopes to prepare the reader for the Bible's account of Satan, whom the ancient Jews and Christians believed to be an existing being but who is not a historical figure in the sense that, for example, Solomon

and Peter were. When we look at biblical accounts of
Satan, we will use modern exegesis, considering the historical situation, the type of written material in which
Satan appears, and the intent of the writer in speaking
about him.

Origins and Development

The greatest modern scholar of Satan is Jeffrey Burton Russell, who wrote a four-volume history of Satan
between 1977 and 1986. In this still-invaluable work,
Russell studied how people understood Satan from ancient Egypt and Mesopotamia to the modern world. He
put much stress on the development of the traditions
about the devil, especially within Christianity.

He proposes "that a concept is *not* best understood in
light of its origins, but rather in light of the direction in
which the tradition is moving." He rejects what he calls
"the genetic fallacy: that the true meaning of a word—or
an idea—lies in its pristine state" (*The Devil*, 49–50).

This is a common notion among historians, but
it is also a Christian idea because Christians believe
that God did not just drop off some revelatory package,
leave us to decipher its contents, and then tell us that
our first understanding of the revelation is normative
for all times. Christians believe that God continues to
act within the community, within the church, and that
ideas and doctrines that emerged later than the Scriptures have validity, although any subsequent development must be grounded in Scripture.

To use a prominent example, the doctrine of the
Trinity as three persons who participate in the one
divine substance or essence is a product of the first
ecumenical council of Nicea of the fourth century and
reflects the theology of the Greek-speaking and Greek-
thinking theologians who produced it. This theological

and doctrinal formulation does not appear in the Bible, but no Christian can envision the faith without the Trinity. In fact, when Nicea proclaimed its teaching, some bishops complained that this teaching was not in Scripture, but the leading theologian of Nicene trinitarianism, Athanasius of Alexandria, replied that the Nicene formula represented the essence of Scripture— that is, the theology of the Trinity grew out of scriptural words and teachings on the Father, Son, and Holy Spirit.

We will take that same approach with Satan and not presume that the devilish figure who first appears in the Bible around 500 BC is the normative Satan for all time. As we shall see, the Jewish idea(s) of Satan kept on developing well after 500 BC, and the Christians, who borrowed heavily from these Jewish ideas, understood Satan as he related to their belief in Jesus Christ—that is, they developed ideas and concepts of Satan that differed from the initial Jewish one but that looked back to it.

Development of ideas and teachings is both normal in Christianity and good for Christianity, protecting it from becoming fossilized and irrelevant to the never-ending numbers of new believers, and development is still going on in the twenty-first century.

CHAPTER TWO

The Problem of Evil in the Old Testament

For religious people, and especially monotheists such as Jews and Christians, the problem of evil has no exact solution. Here, following the Bible and using the masculine for God, the problem of evil sets up this way:

> There is one God.
> He is all-good and all-powerful.
> Since he is all-good, he does not wish his created
>   beings, especially humans made in his image
>   and likeness, to suffer evil.
> Since he is all-powerful, he can prevent them from
>   suffering evil.
> Yet they constantly suffer evil.
> Why?

Every generation of believers has had to deal with the problem of evil. The Christian approach to the problem of evil begins with the ancient Israelites who, of course, were not Christian, but whose sacred writings the Christians claim as part of their own heritage. Satan emerges from the ancient search for an answer to the problem of evil.

The Old Testament account of the People Israel starts with Abraham, father of the Jewish people and father of many nations (Gen 12:1-3). When Abraham enters the biblical scene, he is already an adult. In fact, Genesis 17:1 says that when his son Ishmael was born, he was already ninety-nine years old! Regardless of the obvious exaggeration, Abraham had lived a long life as a pagan, and some ancient Near Eastern views would have been part of his thinking.

We do not know what kind of pagan Abraham was, but he came from Mesopotamia, a Greek word meaning "land between two rivers," in this case the Tigris and Euphrates. This area is also known as the Fertile Crescent, and from there emerged some of the earliest civilizations known to history.

Like many other inhabitants of the Fertile Crescent, Abraham was a Semite. In Israelite legend, this term went back to Noah's son Shem (Gen 11:10-26), and the group included some minor peoples like the Edomites and some major ones like the Babylonians and Assyrians.

The ancient Semites practiced polytheism, the veneration of multiple gods. Semitic polytheism was not uniform; different peoples had different traditions. In general, their gods protected them against the forces of *chaos*, a Greek word meaning "disorder." Opposed to chaos was *cosmos*, a Greek word meaning "order," but not just in a sense that everything worked so much as that the will of the gods was obeyed since the good deities brought cosmos to the people.

The cosmos brought by the gods corresponded to that established by the king and that desired by the people: crops grew, herds increased, invaders were kept at bay, and, most important, people had children to inherit their land and preserve their family name. Moreover, the gods often looked and acted like people, while the monsters of chaos did not.

The most famous ancient Semitic story about the gods is the *Enuma Elish*, an account of creation that survives in several versions, most likely originating in ancient Babylon. It has tremendous significance for understanding the ancient world and the Bible, but we can give only an outline here.

Enuma Elish provides the ancient Babylonian view of the world. A female sea monster named Tiamat challenges the authority of the young male sky god Marduk, patron of Babylon. Tiamat represents the power of the salt sea, a threat to the Fertile Crescent. As a female, she also challenges the cosmos of patriarchy—that is, male rule. To the men who governed the ancient world, male rule symbolized order and harmony. Marduk and Tiamat battle, and the male god prevails. He pierces Tiamat's inside—that is, the womb, the source of female power. He also creates the earth from her body, another acknowledgment of female fertility. He establishes the rule of the gods; cosmos triumphs over chaos.

Naturally the ancient Semitic peoples worried about everyday morality. Honest people worried about theft; truthful people worried about liars. But even everyday concerns like those reflected chaos-cosmos: How could there be order when people stole? How could there be harmony when people lied?

The scarcity of written records makes it impossible to track the direct influence of the pagan Semites upon the ancient Israelites, but we can note that the Garden of Eden was the ultimate cosmos: no one worked, no one got sick, no one died. And, of course, all this was ultimately spoiled by a female.

Less directly influential upon the Israelites—but still very important—was ancient Egypt. The southern tip of Israel bordered on Egypt, some of the tribes of Israel had once been enslaved in Egypt, and the pharaohs routinely intervened politically and militarily in Israel and beyond.

The Egyptians believed in *ma'at*, a somewhat all-purpose word that meant order, justice, truth, and balance. Sometimes the Egyptians personified *ma'at* as a goddess. Like the Semites, the ancient Egyptians also worried about daily matters of morality and justice, but they saw *ma'at* as overriding all. Some scholars attribute this partly to Egypt's geographic isolation, surrounded by a desert that made invasions rare and benefitting from the always reliable Nile to overflow and fertilize the land. This peace and prosperity earned Egypt the name "The Gift of the Nile."

Egypt became a state before 3,000 BC, and in the succeeding centuries its religion changed and developed. The polytheistic Egyptians had good and evil gods although, like the Semitic ones, the evil deities never overthrew the good ones who protected the country.

Scholars have avidly pursued the cultural interactions of the ancient Near East, but many religious people have taken little interest in that. For them, God chose Abraham who then believed in one deity and taught his descendants, the People Israel, to do likewise. But that probably was not the case.

For modern believers, monotheism means speculative monotheism—that is, they believe that there is only one God because it does not make sense to have more than one deity. How can there be more than one all-perfect being? Modern believers do disagree on how God revealed himself to us, who brought his message (Jesus, Mohammed, Joseph Smith), and how we should respond to this deity, but there cannot be more than one.

Yet there can also be a practical monotheism, the belief that there is more than one deity, but only one matters, either because he or she is the most powerful or more caring of humans or the patron of our tribe. The technical term for this is *henotheism*.

The Old Testament offers much evidence of this. The Genesis account of the Hebrew Jacob tells how he worked for the father of his first two wives, Leah and Rachel, and of how his father-in-law Laban cheated him. Finally Jacob fled with his family, and his wife Rachel stole her father's household idols, proof not just that Laban venerated such gods but that Rachel thought them worth stealing, and Jacob thought them worth keeping (Gen 31).

A more familiar example comes from the Ten Commandments, the first of which is "I am the LORD your God, who brought you out of the land of Egypt, out of the house of slavery; you shall not have other gods before me" (Exod 20:2-3). By the time of the Exodus, it had been five hundred years—half a millennium—since God called Abraham, and the people still worshipped other gods.

Modern biblical scholars think that the Israelites were not monotheists until at least the reign of David (1000–970 BC), and many think it did not happen until after the Babylonian exile in the sixth century BC. For most ancient Israelites, the problem of evil was not one of explaining why one powerful deity allowed evil because other supernatural beings also existed.

When trying to determine the beliefs of the earliest Israelites, we run into a real problem, namely, no written records. Old Testament exegetes believe that the first written material that was preserved in the Bible was not composed till around 900 BC. That means that the earliest *written* material came after Abraham, Isaac, Jacob, the slavery in Egypt, Moses, Judges such as Samson and Samuel, the Gentile woman Ruth, the first kings, Saul, David, and Solomon, and many other great Israelite figures who lived and died.

Phrased differently, by the time we get written records the religion of Abraham was more than nine hundred years old, and many of Israel's greatest figures had come and gone. This does not mean that the biblical information about them is unreliable, but it does mean that the material was shaped by people who lived after them.

Sometimes it is obvious that later material has been read back into the past. For example, in Jewish tradition Moses composed the biblical book of Leviticus, which has numerous references to the functions of priests, not exactly a major problem in the Sinai desert and actually reflective of the temple priests who, of course, did not exist until Solomon built the temple centuries after Moses' death.

But much of the biblical material preserved some very old ideas, including some possibly dating back to the age of the patriarchs, including information about evil beings.

For the ancient Israelites, there were abundant malignant spirits, such as the Nephilim, a race of giants mentioned in Numbers 13:33; satyrs (Lev 17:7) who looked like goats with hairy, cloven hooves and lived in deserted areas; a female desert spirit named Lilith (Isa 34:14) who later degenerated into a night hag who would kill children if they were not wearing protective amulets; and witches—actually mediums who consulted spirits of the dead and claimed to use those spirits to tell the future. King Saul banished them but later consulted one of them, the Witch of Endor (1 Sam 28:8-19). Following the pagan tradition of the sea monster Tiamat, the Israelites had Behemoth, Leviathan, and Rahab (Job 40:15; 3:8; 9:13).

In addition to these legendary beings, there were the pagan gods whom many Israelites thought to be real, which is why the prophets always railed against idolatry.

But nowhere in the Old Testament is there is a devil as we understand him today.

On the other hand, the picture of God from this period is not one that modern believers would feel comfortable with. He often set good and evil in terms of ritual and/or legal purity, and he had no mercy for the innocent. When the Israelites, God's chosen people, captured Jericho, they killed everyone in the city, including newborn infants, except for the family of a prostitute who had helped Israelite spies. When they captured the city of Ai, no one was spared. We have already seen how in the account of the tenth plague God killed all the firstborn children of Egypt, including those who had done no harm to the Hebrews. When David and Bathsheba committed adultery and she became pregnant, God punished the *adulterers* by killing the *child* (2 Sam 12:15-18).

Not just the innocent but even people who did what we would think is the right thing were punished.

Second Samuel 6 tells of how King David had the ark of the covenant brought to Jerusalem on a cart guided by two men named Uzzah and Ahio, whom we would today call lay people because they did not have a sacred calling. "When they came to the threshing floor of Nacon, Uzzah reached out his hand to the ark of God and took hold of it, for the oxen shook it. The anger of the LORD was kindled against Uzzah; and God struck him there because he reached out his hand to the ark; and he died there beside the ark of God" (6:6-7). Uzzah, not being a priest, was not allowed to touch the ark, but we naturally wonder, what was he supposed to do? Let the ark fall on the ground and be damaged?

There is no answer to that question because our attitude differs so much from the ancient one, but this episode does show how violation of ritual purity was considered a great sin, one even worthy of death.

The ancient Israelite view of God appears best in Isaiah 45:7 where God says, "I form light and create darkness, I make weal and create woe; I the LORD do all these things." This is a difficult and debatable passage. On the one hand, it proclaims God as the creator of *all*, regardless of whether humans consider some of his creations to be evil. On the other hand, it could make God responsible for evil, and some scholars, especially Jeffrey Russell (*The Devil* 176–81), believe that this is the verse's intention. For the earliest Israelites, God combined in himself both good and evil. This sounds strange at first, but often in ancient religions deities combined opposites in themselves. Recall that Genesis 1:27 says, "God created humankind in his image . . . male and female he created them." Note that God's image combines two opposites, female and male, so it is quite possible that early ideas of God did picture him combining in his person both good and evil.

But, along with an emphasis on ritual purity, this ambiguous view of God faded before a new conception of goodness promoted by the Israelite prophets.

The prophets appeared early, during the reign of Saul (1020–1000 BC), and they would be a feature of Israelite life right down to John the Baptist. The prophets claimed to speak for God and to have been inspired by him. If the people believed the prophets' claims, then they had great power, even enough to rebuke a king, as the prophet Nathan did when David arranged for the death of Uriah, the husband of his mistress Bathsheba (1 Sam 12:1-12).

But the prophets' real interest lay not in personal morality but in social justice. Amos denounced those who "trample on the needy, and bring to ruin the poor of the land . . . buying the poor for silver and the needy for a pair of sandals" (Amos 8:4, 6). Isaiah denounced the royal court and the city of Jerusalem's leaders. "Everyone loves a bribe and runs after gifts. They do not defend the orphan, and the widow's cause does not come before them" (Isa 1:23).

Stung by the criticism, the leaders defended themselves. Falling back on ritual purity, they pointed to their participation in religious festivals and their support of the cults. Significantly, the prophet Amos turned that traditional argument on its head. What good is it to go through the motions when people have evil hearts: "I [God] hate, I despise your festivals, and I take no delight in your solemn assemblies" (Amos 5:21).

The prophet Micah asked, "Will the LORD be pleased with thousands of rams [for sacrifice], with ten thousands of rivers of oil? . . . what does the Lord require of you but to do justice, and to love kindness?" (Mic 6:7-8).

Isaiah phrased it most forcefully:

bringing offerings is futile;
   incense is an abomination to me. . . .
I cannot endure solemn assemblies with iniquity. . . .
Wash yourselves; make yourselves clean;
   remove the evil of your doings
   from before my eyes;
cease to do evil,
   learn to do good;
seek justice,
   rescue the oppressed,
defend the orphan,
   plead for the widow. (1:13-17)

The prophets were not naïve. They knew the powerful would continue to oppress the poor and the weak and that most people would continue to measure their religiosity by going to the temple rather than by how they treated others. But the prophets had great moral authority, and over the centuries they managed to change the Israelite view not just of what God wanted people to do but also of who God was. God still wanted people to follow ritual and cultic purity, but care for the deprived and weak now took precedence. That in turn meant that God could no longer be seen as the ruthless avenger of every petty violation of cultic or ritual purity. Furthermore, the prophets emphasized the essential goodness of God, and by the sixth century BC, they and the writers influenced by them had abandoned portraying God in a morally dubious way.

Yet people still sinned and violated the moral and cultic codes. God may not have been attacking mortals anymore, but these people did deserve punishment.

But if God would not inflict it, then who would?

Enter Satan.

As we saw, the earliest Israelites practiced henotheism, venerating one deity but without eliminating the possibility of others. Even as the Israelites moved toward monotheism, they did not consider that God reigned alone. Several biblical passages (1 Kgs 19, Ps 82, Job 1) speak of a divine "royal court" with God surrounded by the *bene ha-elohim* or "Sons of God." The Bible also speaks of divine messengers whom God sent to earth to make announcements or to carry out his will. In Hebrew they are called *mal'ak*; in Greek they are *ángeloi* (*ángelos* in the singular) from which we get the English word "angel."

(*Since almost the beginning of Christian art, angels have been portrayed as human beings wearing white cloaks and possessing large wings, which enable them to transport themselves to and from heaven. In fact, neither the Old Testament nor the New ever describes the appearance of an angel.*)

These lesser spiritual beings had great authority. The People Israel came into being during the Exodus, which was prompted by God's speaking to Moses from the burning bush, telling him to return to Egypt and demand that Pharaoh "Let my people go." But when we read the biblical account, we find (Exod 3:2): "There an *angel* of the LORD appeared to him in a flame of fire

out of a bush." Given the awesome consequences for
the People Israel of the calling of Moses, the fact that
an angel appeared to him makes it clear how significant
such a being was to the ancient Israelites.

But not all divine messengers brought positive news.
Often in the Old Testament God acts harshly—and not
just against pagans like Pharaoh and the Canaanites
whom Israel conquered. The great king David (ca. 1002
– ca. 970 BC) was so loved by God that he was called
"God's Anointed," translated into Greek as *Christós*.
But even David offended God. At one point "the anger
of the LORD was kindled against Israel, and he incited
David against them, saying, 'Go, count [census] the
people of Israel and Judah'" (2 Sam 24:1). This was a
forbidden act, and even though God turned David to
it, he still held it against David for taking the census.
(This is a good example of the problems the traditional
view of the deity could cause.) Since David had sinned,
God had to discipline him, but he gave David a choice
of three punishments. The king chose a three-day pestilence over the land of Israel. An angel carried out the
punishment, spreading pestilence everywhere, being
stopped by God only when the angel had turned toward
destroying the holy city of Jerusalem (2 Sam 24:15-17).

Traditionally, God had been content to carry out
harsh punishments himself, but the prophetic view
of an all-good deity made the this approach less valid
and certainly less appealing to the people, even when
what God did was clearly in the right. More and more
the "dirty work" was passed to the angels, and not just
in the Old Testament. Consider the angels of the New
Testament Apocalypse who blew their trumpets and let
loose vast destruction on the world (Rev 8:6-12).

The most dangerous of these divine punishers was a
satan. This sounds puzzling: "a satan"? That is because
we normally think of Satan, an individual figure with a

proper name, but that was not the case in the Old Testament. The Hebrew phrase *ho satan* means "the adversary" or "accuser," which are not negative terms. Acting like a prosecutor, the satan accuses people of sins before God. In several places in the Old Testament, the word appears as a verb, as in "to play the satan." In fact, the earliest appearance of the word is as a verb.

In the book of Numbers a pagan king of Moab, justly fearful of the invading Israelites, sent messengers to a wizard named Balaam, asking, "Come now, curse this people for me, since they are stronger than I" (22:6). After first refusing the request, Balaam finally agreed. God naturally protected his chosen people, and he sent an angel who "plays the Satan" (22:22; my translation) and prevents Balaam from aiding the pagans.

Additionally, in an account of Solomon's reign in 1 Kings, the word "satan" is used twice for pagan kings whom God raised up to challenge Solomon to punish him for his sins (1 Kgs 11:14, 23).

In only three Old Testament books does the word "Satan" appear as a proper noun: the books of Zechariah, 1 Chronicles, and Job. All three are comparatively late, written after the Jewish leaders, who had been exiled by the Babylonians and had been freed by the Persian king Cyrus after his conquest of Babylonia in 539, returned to their homeland. Most scholars date these books to 500 BC, or at least to the fifth century BC.

In the book of Zechariah, the prophet has a vision of "the high priest Joshua standing before the angel of the Lord, and Satan at his right hand to accuse him. And the LORD said to Satan, 'The LORD rebuke you, O Satan!'" (3:1-2). Why? Because Satan had misjudged Joshua and thought he had sinned. Note that Satan stands in the presence of the Lord along with the angel, and the Lord does not rebuke him for doing evil but for being too zealous a prosecutor.

The Chronicler is a name scholars give to an anonymous writer who, in two volumes titled 1–2 Chronicles, rewrote much of the history of David and the kings of Israel and Judah, which had been recorded in the earlier books 1–2 Samuel and 1–2 Kings. In general, the Chronicler presents a very favorable view of David, by that time widely venerated among the Jews as their greatest king and founder of the royal dynasty. (Recall that the gospel writer Matthew pointed out that Jesus came from the House of David in his genealogy of Jesus at the beginning of his gospel.)

The Chronicler retold the story of the pestilence. In 2 Samuel 24, God punished David for carrying out the census that God himself had incited David to take. By the fifth century this view of God seemed dated and offensive, so the Chronicler simply changed the account: "Satan stood up against Israel, and incited David to count the people of Israel" (1 Chr 21:1). Note that Satan does not here act as an adversary but instead does something evil. Yet, for some inexplicable reason, God does not stop him from doing it, probably because the Chronicler was less interested in Satan than in exonerating God.

The last and most important Old Testament reference to Satan as a proper noun occurs in the book of Job, the Bible's foremost *theodicy*.

"Theodicy" is a term coined by the great German philosopher Gottfried Wilhelm von Leibniz (1646–1716). The word comes from two Greek words, *theós* meaning "God" and *diké* meaning "righteousness." What a theodicy does is to *attempt* to reconcile the coexistence of a good and powerful deity and of evil, the question with which this chapter began. Theodicy does not solve the problem of evil because the relation of God to evil is a mystery—that is, something that is beyond understanding but with which believers must deal. (A parallel would be how Jesus can be both divine and human—a matter of faith but also a mystery of faith since it is beyond human comprehension.)

Every religious group must deal with evil, and primitive theodicies survive from the ancient world, including a prominent Babylonian one about a man who dutifully worships the gods but still suffers, a tale that may have been known to the Israelites. But the one that stands out is the book of Job, written by an anonymous Jew in the fifth century BC. It is one the greatest treasures bequeathed by the ancient Jews to later generations.

This fictional book contains an important treatment of Satan, but first, here is a basic outline of the book and its theodicy.

The book opens with God holding court: "One day heavenly beings came to present themselves before the Lord, and Satan also came among them" (1:6). God points out to Satan that his servant Job loves and reveres him. Satan replies that God has given him children, land, and herds, so it is no wonder that Job loves God. Satan then challenges God to take everything away from Job and see what happens.

God agrees, and Satan proceeds to destroy Job's wealth, then kill all his children, and finally afflict Job with sores over all his body, but the steadfast Job does not curse God, instead uttering the famous words, "The Lord gave, and the Lord has taken away; blessed be the name of the Lord" (Job 1:21).

Job suffered, but he was innocent. According to the traditional theodicy of Judaism, God imposed suffering on only the wicked. Thus three friends of Job, horrified at what had happened to him but convinced that Job must have sinned to have suffered so much, go to him to try to convince him to admit his guilt so he could be reconciled with God. In dozens of chapters of brilliant poetry, the friends make their argument, and

Job refutes them. Another man comes along with a vari-
ant on the traditional argument, but Job refutes him as
well.

Job says, "Here is my signature! Let the Almighty answer me!" (31:35). To his amazement, God does.

Basically God proclaims that Job cannot understand
the divine nature. For the author of Job, God is simply beyond human ability to comprehend. We cannot
understand why God acts how he does, and this remains a mystery and a problem for us. Job accepts this:
"I have uttered what I did not understand, things too
wonderful for me, which I did not know" (42:3). Such a
conclusion—acceptance of the mystery of divine activity—does not rest well with modern people who have
access to unbelievable amounts of information and who
strive to understand almost anything, but on the question of evil, the author of Job may be right.

Yet important and compelling as this theodicy is, we
must focus on the picture of Satan, the longest in the
Old Testament, even though he actually appears only in
the first two chapters of Job.

Note that Satan is not in hell but in heaven. Satan
says that he has been going about the earth (1:7). Why?
Many scholars believe—since Job was written in the
Persian period—that Satan here acts like Persian officials
called "the eyes of the King," that is, they traveled about
the empire to check to make sure all was well and to re-
port problems or problematic people to the king.

God asks Satan if he has seen Job who is "blameless
and upright." Satan says yes but then asks the questions
we just noted—would Job still fear God if the Deity had
not treated him so well? The adversary has just made a
challenge.

In the book, God accepts Satan's challenge, which,
of course, he does not have to do. He is the Deity, he
knows what is in Job's heart, and he does not need to

subject him to such a barbarous test. But this is fiction, and so God allows Satan to try to prove his point, which he fails to do.

God has proved his own terrible point, and, by all rights, Satan should now back off. Indeed, as one of the sons of God, he should be pleased that this human maintains his loyalty to God in spite of horrific suffering. If this were the case, Satan would remain the adversary.

But Satan does not back off. He insists upon a second test, inflicting disease upon Job's body, which God permits and which produces the same results. While Satan remains the divine servant and is not expelled from the heavenly court, he shows signs of evil. He does not accept the divine victory, humbly and fairly acknowledging that God was right about Job. Instead he acts independently, insisting on another trial with no concern about putting poor Job through more suffering. Granted, Satan can act only with the divine permission, but this incipient independence would grow among the ancient Jews.

If these three passages (Zechariah, 1 Chronicles, and Job) are the only Old Testament ones that treat of Satan, what about the most famous account of Satan in the Old Testament, namely, in the Garden of Eden?

For the ancient Israelites, the book of Genesis really began with the story of Abraham, whose history starts at 11:10 with the descendants of Shem, one of Noah's sons and the ancestor of all the Semites. Genesis then traces the history of Abraham, his son Isaac, his sons Esau and Jacob (who is also called Israel), and the twelve sons of Jacob—that is, the founders of the Twelve Tribes of Israel.

To this account, which continues in one form or another through five books (the *Torah*) to the death of Moses (Deuteronomy 34), an anonymous editor added a preface, a brief world history that started with the creation and went through to the tower of Babel and the descendants of Shem.

Genesis 1–11 stands apart from the rest of the book and has had a long and spectacular life of its own. It consists of the creation of the world in six days, the Garden of Eden, Adam, Eve, the temptation and Fall, the expulsion from Eden, and the children of the first couple, starting with Cain and Abel and going on to the descendants of their third son Seth, which ends at chapter 5. Chapter 6 opens with a strange passage about heavenly beings, which we still study in detail, then it goes on to Noah and the Flood, which runs through to the descendants of Noah in chapter 10. This preface to the Israelite history ends with the tower of Babel.

Because of Pauline theology, the doctrine of original sin, and modern fundamentalism and creationism, the opening chapters of Genesis have garnered unlimited attention among Christians. But the story had little impact on the ancient Israelites. Outside of Genesis 1–11, Adam appears only once in the entire Hebrew Bible. In the opening verse of 1 Chronicles, at the beginning of a massive genealogy, we read "Adam, Seth, Enosh, Kenan, Mahalalel. . . ." Literally, Adam is just a name. As for Eve, she appears nowhere else in the Hebrew Bible. The ancient Israelites just did not consider the Garden of Eden very important.

But what about Satan? Actually the Genesis account of Adam and Eve, the Garden, and the forbidden fruit never uses the word "Satan." It refers only to a serpent. Later writers, both Jewish (Wis 2:24) and Christian (Rev 12:9; 20:12) identified the serpent as Satan (as did non-biblical writers), but Genesis itself does not. What then does Genesis say?

The Garden of Eden represents another ancient story of cosmos and chaos. The Hebrew god created a perfect place—literally a garden in the middle of a desert region—and filled it with all kinds of living creatures, including two special ones made in his image and likeness. These two creatures, called humans, lived like children: they had no conception of work, of illness, of death. All they had to do was obey the father figure's commands. But, like all children, they went through a period of adolescent rebellion, disobeying their father. Like adolescents, they also became sexually aware. But they soon found out that growing up, no matter how much fun it may bring, also demands responsibilities. They must work for a living, and their father literally kicks them out of the house so that they, like adults, must fend for themselves, although they continue to have their father's love.

The Eden narrative also has a strong patriarchal element. The serpent deceives Eve, not Adam, who simply gives in to Eve. Note that when God is reproaching Adam, the *first* thing he says to him is, "Because you have listened to the voice of your wife . . ." (3:17). This story of human beginnings has many parallels to other creation myths. Perhaps the one best known in Western culture would be the Greek myth of Pandora, the primeval woman who spoils the perfect world for everyone else by disobeying a command.

The serpent symbolizes chaos, and not just here. Tiamat, the Babylonian monster, was a sea serpent. In Greek mythology the hero Cadmus battles a dragon so he could found the city of Thebes. In Nordic mythology, the god Thor battles against the Midgard Serpent whose coils stretch around the world. It is no surprise that the ancient Israelites also had a cosmos/chaos myth with a serpent in it. Consider Isaiah 27:1: "In that day the Lord with his cruel and great and strong sword will punish Leviathan the fleeing serpent, Leviathan the twisting serpent, and he will kill the dragon that is in the sea."

A dragon, of course, is basically a large serpent.

(The book of Isaiah also recalls the Genesis cosmos/chaos element when God promises "For I am about to create a new heaven and new earth" [65:17]).

But if the Genesis text says "serpent" and nothing more, why do so many Christians believe that the serpent was Satan? Because later generations of Jews believed it to be so, and the Christians picked it up from them.

Before moving on to those writers, let us reconsider what the Old Testament says about Satan. Basically, very little. As noted, Satan or "the satan" appears as a personal figure only three times, in 1 Chronicles, Zechariah, and Job, all books written after 500 BC, that is, in the Persian period quite late in Israelite history. For more than a millennium from the call of Abraham—a period that includes Moses, Joshua, David, Solomon, Isaiah, Jeremiah, and a host of other great figures—the ancient Israelites literally had no Satan as a personal being.

Nor did the word necessarily have negative connotations. Satan acted as an adversary, working alongside an angel in Zechariah and being in the heavenly court in Job. He was surely an unattractive figure but not an evil one. Nor was he a resident of hell because that concept had not yet arisen, as we shall soon see.

We also have to ask why the three Old Testament books that mention Satan were written after 500 BC.

Throughout their history, the Jews had been involved with Egypt and the great Semitic states of the ancient Near East, specifically Assyria and Babylonia. In 597 and again in 587 BC, the Babylonians attacked Judea and carried its leaders back to Babylon. There the leaders and many of their followers remained until 539—the "Babylonian captivity." But during this period a new power had arisen in the East, non-African and non-Semitic. This was Persia, led by the brilliant king Cyrus the Great (559–530 BC). In 539 Cyrus captured Babylon and allowed the Jewish leaders to return home. Most but not all did.

Unlike many ancient rulers, Cyrus did not insist that his subjects follow his religion. The book of Isaiah (44:28) actually says that Cyrus encouraged the Jews to rebuild the Jerusalem temple, which the Babylonians had destroyed. This prophetic book even referred to him as "the Lord's Anointed," which would be *Messiah* in Hebrew and *Christós* in Greek.

The Persians would rule the Jews for just over two centuries, ceding rule in 333 to the Macedonian king Alexander the Great (356–323), but virtually nothing certain is known about the Jews under Persian rule. It is, however, very likely that Persian influence helped to establish the now familiar image of Satan.

Religiously the Persians were Zoroastrian dualists, that is, they believed in two deities: a good one, Ahura Mazda, and an evil one, Ahriman. The Persians did not impose this on the Jews, but two centuries of contact with Zoroastrians certainly made the Jews aware of a tradition that sharply separated a good being from an evil one. It is likely that this impacted their views of Satan. The Jews kept their monotheism but, probably under Persian influence, they emphasized the role of Satan and began to separate him from the good God of Israel, thus explaining why the only three Old Testament books that mention Satan as a person all date from the Persian period and why the much magnified role of Satan among the Jews occurred after that same period.

Cyrus was something of a visionary, seeing one deity, known under a variety of names, ruling the world. With Alexander the Great, the Jews found themselves under another visionary king who brought not a new deity but a new and powerful culture, that of Greece, which would influence Jewish ideas on Satan and on the afterlife.

So before turning to this new culture, let us see what the ancient Jews before Alexander believed about an afterlife, especially for sinners.

Naturally the ancient Jews wondered about the possibility of postmortem existence. They never really formulated a specific doctrine, but many believed in a place called *Sheol*, which appears more than sixty times in the Old Testament and is usually translated into English as simply the "abode of the dead."

Typically, to get to *Sheol*, one had to go down, putting *Sheol* in the bottom of the Old Testament three-decker universe, that is, heaven above, earth in the middle, and the underworld below. The Old Testament references to *Sheol* characterize it as dark, silent, and dusty (Job 17:16). Some texts present a very negative image: Isaiah 14:11 refers to maggots and worms in *Sheol*.

The earliest references to *Sheol* are somewhat ambiguous, but over the centuries the images took on clearer lines. *Sheol* has gates (Isa 38:10; Ps 9:14; Job 38:17), and no one can ever leave it.

Sheol was often referred to as the Pit (Ps 16:10; 49:10; Job 33:22). The question often came up about the relation of those in *Sheol* to God: "In Sheol who can give you praise?" (Ps 6:5); those who are there cannot praise God or affirm their faithfulness to him (Isa 38:17). The notion that those in *Sheol* were fully separated from God would cause problems that Jews of the postbiblical period would take up.

Although not a place of eternal punishment, *Sheol* was the place to which God sent the wicked, sometimes even before they died. In the book of Numbers, God deals harshly with Korah, a man who defied Moses. "The ground under them was split apart. The earth opened its mouth and swallowed them up. . . . So they with all that belonged to them went down alive into Sheol" (16:31-33). Upon arrival in *Sheol*, they were forever dead.

One movement in the direction of the Christian hell appeared in the book of the prophet Ezekiel in the sixth century BC. It bothered the Jews that there was no distinction in *Sheol* between the good and the evil. Starting with the Egyptians, Ezekiel and later writers distinguished the wicked from the good in *Sheol*: "They have come down, they lie still, the uncircumcised, killed by the sword" (32:21). Other enemies of Israel met the same fate, being thrust directly into *Sheol* and without a proper burial, a serious matter since lack of a tomb and a proper burial constituted a significant disgrace in the ancient Near East.

Definitely not a place of reward for the blessed but neither was *Sheol* a place only for punishment of the wicked. (Some modern Bibles translate the word as "hell," but that is anachronistic.) In general it was a place after death, at best undesirable but of not one of punishment. Regarding life after death, the anonymous author of Ecclesiastes drily summed it up this way: "A living dog is better than a dead lion" (9:4).

And at no point in the Old Testament was Satan a resident of *Sheol*.

Alexander the Great has fascinated people for generations as the man who brought Greek culture to the Near East, a bit of an idealization since he brought that culture with his army. But there is no doubt that he effected a major cultural change, although not personally. He died at age 33 in 323, and no one person could govern the new empire he had created, so his generals began carving out sections for themselves in an area that stretched from Macedonia to India. Two of these empires would impact the Jews.

A general named Ptolemy obtained a kingdom in Egypt, centered in the city of Alexandria; the Ptolemaic dynasty survived until the suicide of Cleopatra in 31 BC. Another general named Seleucus established a kingdom in the Near East, a state that included the Jews; his dynasty survived until the middle of the first century BC.

These two dynasties faced a major problem: vast foreign civilizations that had to be ruled by outsiders. Naturally the monarchs took the usual political and economic steps to govern, but they also took a novel approach of introducing a new culture to the Near East, Greek culture. Scholars call this process "Hellenization," that is, "to make Greek." It had great impact on the Jews in the period scholars call Hellenistic.

Immediately after Alexander's death, his successors fought over territory, and much of the fighting occurred in Judea, which was devastated. By the year 300 many Jews had begun to migrate out of their homeland in search of a better life. Many went to Alexandria, which soon had a large, well-educated, and prosperous Jewish community that made up at least 20 percent of the city's population and possibly more. The Alexandrian Jews soon adopted Greek as their everyday language and then, to the chagrin of traditionalists, for their religion as well. Starting in the third century they began translating the Bible into Greek, a translation known as the *Septuagint* (itself a Greek word). One of the words translated into Greek was "Satan," and the translation *diábolos* gave us the word "devil."

Not all Jews went to Alexandria. Some went to Syria, others to Asia Minor (modern Turkey), and, by the second century BC, to Rome. The presence of the Jews outside their homeland is called the *Diasporá*, the Greek word for "dispersion." Probably the most famous diasporan Jew was the apostle Paul.

Surely the greatest impact of Greek thought on the Jews was the strong belief in life after death and especially with the status of the deceased dependent on their lives on earth, usually in the form of rewards and punishments, rather than the mere continued existence characteristic of *Sheol*. Significantly, punishment was purely retributive and included no attempt to reform the sinner. The gods avenged the offences the evil ones had committed during their lifetimes. With no hope of change, the sinners suffered most from despair. The Christian concept of hell would generally follow these lines.

Among the Greeks, life for the blessed deceased was not much better. In *The Odyssey* of Homer (11.488–491), Odysseus goes into the underworld where he meets the great Greek warrior Achilles. Odysseus praises Achilles's great achievements when he was alive and lauds him as a prince of the dead. Achilles replies that he would rather be the slave of the poorest peasant in the world than ruler of the dead if he could only be alive again, a parallel to Ecclesiastes' live dog and dead lion.

But not all Greeks held such a pessimistic view. The philosopher Plato (424–347 BC) considered the body "the prison of the soul" (*Phaedo*, 62b) from which one could escape at death.

We cannot be sure when the Jews began moving toward a belief in an afterlife of rewards and punishments, but Greek influence pushed them in that direction. Now God could posthumously reward the good who had suffered in this life and punish the wicked, in effect evening the score. Belief in an afterlife certainly made life—and God—look more fair.

Belief in a blessed afterlife appears in one biblical book, Daniel, written around the middle of the second century when the Seleucid kings of Syria were persecuting the Jews. One king in particular, Antiochus IV

(175–164 BC), attacked not only the Jews but also their religion, eventually provoking a revolt led by a family called the Maccabees. This revolt liberated the country for a century before the Roman conquest of 63 BC.

Daniel is an early example of apocalyptic litera-ture. *Apokálypsis* is the Greek word for revelation, and apocalyptic writers claimed to have divine inspiration for their works. Apocalyptic includes a variegated range of literature, but basically it deals with a fundamental problem: why have God's chosen people suffered so? The basic apocalyptic answer is that the deity has been biding his time and will come in power at the end of the age to wreak vengeance upon the evildoers and, very importantly, to reward the faithful by restoring his king-dom but also by providing them with a blessed afterlife.

The book 2 Maccabees, accepted by the Orthodox and Roman Catholic churches as Scripture but not by Jews or Protestants, was written in Greek around 100 BC, most likely by a diasporan Jew in Alexandria. In its seventh chapter the book speaks openly about the resur-rection of the dead. This book did not have much influ-ence among the Jews in Palestine, and it may reflect the strong impact of Greek culture on the Alexandrian Jews, but it was widely read by Christians.

This book's approach made much sense religiously. Many of the good people would die before the end of the age and would never benefit from God's apocalyptic coming. The author of Daniel wrote during a period when many Jews had died for their religion, while 2 Maccabees explicitly deals with martyrs. If God is just, was there no reward for these brave Jews who per-ished for their faith in this one true God?

The slow but steady growth of a belief in a blessed afterlife made *Sheol* less acceptable. The realm of God had always existed; now there was need for a realm for the deceased wicked. By 200 BC the Jews had begun to use the word *Gehenna* as a place for the eternal suffering of the damned. The name derives from the valley of Hinnon just south of Jerusalem. It was a place of human sacrifice where children were offered to the pagan deity Moloch, not just by pagans but by wicked Jewish kings such as Ahaz and Manasseh (2 Chr 28:3; 33:6). The use of this term became widespread and was even used by Jesus (Matt 5:22; 18:9). It became the model for the Christian notion of hell, the perpetual residence of Satan. (The English word "hell" dates to the eighth century.)

CHAPTER THREE

Jewish Apocryphal Literature

So far we have been tracing Satan through Jewish biblical literature, but there is much other ancient Jewish
literature. Of great importance is apocryphal literature.
Basically, "apocryphal" means books claiming to be by
or about biblical figures but which have not been accepted into the biblical *canon* or official list of books.
In the plural these books are called *apócrypha*, a Greek
word; *apócryphon* is the word for a single book.

"Apocryphal" is not a negative term. Every religion
has enormous numbers of worthwhile books that are
not in the religion's sacred writings. For example, Christians still read *The Imitation of Christ* by Thomas
à Kempis (ca. 1380–1471) and *The Pilgrim's Progress* by
John Bunyan (1628–1688) for the spiritual content—
probably of far more benefit to them than reading the
legal material in the biblical book of Leviticus. But the
apocryphal books claim a unique importance by being
contemporary with the biblical books or written not
long after them. Often believers do not know that some
of their most cherished stories are not found in the
Bible but in these noncanonical books instead.

Let me give examples from Christian apocrypha. A
mid-second-century work from Syria titled *The Proto-*

gospel of James recounts that the parents of Jesus' mother Mary were named Anna and Joachim. The *Acts of Peter* from second-century Asia Minor tells of Saint Peter's crucifixion in Rome. People who have rarely or even never read the Bible may know of the stories of Mary's parents and Peter's crucifixion.

The Jewish apocrypha became prominent in the third century BC, and several of them have important accounts of Satan and other beings referred to as *diábolos* and *daímon*.

The Greek word *diábolos* was used by the Jewish translators of the Old Testament for the Hebrew word *Satan*, which, as we saw in the previous chapter, became the root word for "devil" in several European languages.

The Greek word *daímon* had a complex history. It did not originally have a negative meaning. The epic poet Homer actually applied the word to Zeus, king of the Greek pantheon. But gradually the Greeks understood the demons to be lesser deities, active on earth, but not negative ones. The Greek philosopher Plato recounts how his teacher Socrates had a *daímon* who sometimes inspired him. But by the time the Jewish apocryphal literature was being written, the word signified a minor evil spirit, which is how it was used by the Jewish writers.

The Jews and the earliest Christians preserved the distinction between devil and demon, often seeing the former as one person who led the evil enterprise, while the latter was a term for lesser evil beings, often followers of the devil. By the Middle Ages this distinction had largely disappeared, and we can read of "devils" in the plural and see Satan described as a demon.

But, for monotheists, the existence of these creatures presented a problem. Where did they come from? God creates all, and he can only create what is good. Gradually the Jews and then the Christians would accept that Satan and the demons had once been angels but, using the free will given to them by God, had sinned their way out of heaven. The "Fall of the Angels," as this came to be known, does not have a strong biblical foundation but does appear in the apocrypha.

The apocrypha were read and used by ancient Jews, including the earliest followers of Jesus. The New Testament Epistle of Jude cites two Jewish apocryphal books, *1 Enoch* and *Assumption of Moses*, and makes allusions to other apocryphal works. In a similar vein, the apostle Paul passed along a rabbinic legend about a rock that followed the Israelites through the desert on the Exodus (1 Cor 10:4). If we restrict ourselves to just the biblical books, we would not learn much about ancient notions of the devil or of many other matters.

The apocryphal books can rarely be dated exactly, but scholars have been able to come up with approximate dates. However, what is most important is that the notions of evil (and many other religious matters) in those books were current during the period (50–125) when Christian writers composed what we now call the New Testament.

The most important Jewish apocryphon is *1 Enoch*, a composite work most likely written in Palestine. Its earliest sections date to the second century BC, while the later ones date to the first century BC. It was originally written in Aramaic, a Semitic dialect widely used for daily affairs and by Jesus when he preached. The New Testament preserves fragments of his Aramaic words, such as *talithá cum* ("Little girl, stand up") and *ĕphphata* ("Be opened"), both from Mark's gospel (5:41; 7:34). But *1 Enoch* does not survive *in toto* in its original language—for example, much is in Ethiopic— yet scholars have successfully reconstructed the book.

These apocryphal books often had an apocalyptic quality, that is, they had either direct or symbolic warnings about the end of the age as does the New Testament book of Revelation, to use the most famous example. Often the books focus upon the struggle between good and evil, usually in the form of a conflict between beneficent and malignant spirits. They also, like Revelation, take an interest in how the world began as a complement to the accounts of the end.

In the Old Testament Enoch appears only in chapter 5 of Genesis (although, like Adam, he is mentioned in the opening chapter of 1 Chronicles and is also just a name there). Enoch forms a link in the generations from Adam to Noah. The first reference to him is standard genealogy: "When Jared had lived one hundred sixty-two years he became the father of Enoch. Jared lived after the birth of Enoch eight hundred years, and he had other sons and daughters. Thus all the days of Jared were nine hundred sixty-two years; and he died" (Gen 5:18-20).

Enoch follows a similar pattern but with a much shorter lifespan: "When Enoch had lived sixty-five years, he became the father of Methuselah. Enoch walked with God after the birth of Methuselah three hundred years, and he had other sons and daughters. Thus all the days of Enoch were three hundred sixty-five years" (5:21-23). The number of his years corresponds to the days of the year, and Enoch was seventh generation of Adam, the number seven corresponding to the sacred day, the Sabbath, on which the Lord rested after the six days of creation (Gen 2:1-3). Clearly these numbers relate to the calendar. Considering the fondness for astrology in the ancient Near East, these numbers, especially 365, may reflect pagan influences. One thing is sure: for the ancient Jews, Enoch clearly represented someone more than just a descendant of Adam.

Then comes a puzzling reference: "Enoch walked with God; then he was no more, because God took him" (5:24). The phrase "walked with God" implies that he did not die but was taken up into heaven. This interpretation was widely accepted by ancient Jews. Around 200 BC, Sirach, a Jewish author whose work is accepted into the Old Testament canon of Catholics and Orthodox, said of him, "Enoch pleased the Lord and was taken up" (44:16), and "Few have ever been created on earth like Enoch, for he was taken up from the earth" (49:14).

Additionally, the Christian biblical writer Jude (v. 14) credited Enoch with prophetic abilities.

As one who had been taken up by God and had the ability to prophesy, Enoch made the perfect literary spokesman for later writers.

First Enoch is a long, diverse book, but we will focus primarily on its significance for the development of the idea of the devil. Since all of the book's contents would have been known in the New Testament era, we will not distinguish the earlier from the later parts of *1 Enoch*.

The book starts with yet another puzzling Genesis passage: "When people began to multiply on the face of the ground, and daughters were born to them, the sons of God saw that they were fair; and they took wives for themselves of all that they chose. . . . The Nephilim were on the earth in those days—and also afterward— when the sons of God went in to the daughters of humans, who bore children to them. These were the heroes that were of old, warriors of renown" (Gen 6:1-2, 4). In the book of Numbers (13:33) the Nephilim are identified as a race of giants, and the word "Nephilim" is linguistically linked to a Semitic word for "fallen," probably because they either fell from heaven or are the offspring of fallen heavenly beings.

Slowly but surely Jewish authors understood the sons of God as angels. The first-century Jewish historian Josephus says it outright: "Many of the angels of God united with women" (cited by Forsyth, 158).

Modern scholars see this strange story as a piece of mythology that somehow found its way into the Genesis narrative, but the ancient Jews took it very seriously. Since the sons of God could not have lusted after the daughters of men without having looked down from heaven at them, the Jews referred to them as the Watcher Angels and saw little good in them as *1 Enoch* demonstrates.

The book opens with Enoch recounting the wonders of creation and the acts of God to his son Methuselah. The Watchers appear in the very first chapter. In what would become a standard understanding of the creation narrative among Christians, Enoch says that the Watchers' leader Semyaza wanted to mate with the earth women—something that would anger God—and feared that the other angels would let him suffer for it, so he got them to bind themselves with oaths and curses to go along with him. They did, and Watcher angels descended to earth and had relations with the women, who gave birth to a race of violent giants. Significantly *1 Enoch* speaks of the Watchers bringing evil to earth but not of evil human beings.

Azazel, another Watcher and possibly a patron of metallurgists, taught the men of earth how to make weapons. He also taught women how to beautify themselves with gold and silver jewelry as well as how to use makeup. (Later Christian writers explained this— unchronologically—by saying that the Watchers did not realize that the women would age, and when that happened, they taught the women how to use makeup!)

Already we find some basics of the later devil accounts. The evil angels start out in heaven but commit a sin that prevents them from returning there. Note also that they teach humans to do evil things, reminiscent of the Fall in Eden, but the fallen angels did not initiate evil on earth since their story appears in Genesis 6, well after the disobedience of Adam and Eve and Cain's murder of his brother Abel. But the Watcher Angels did abet humans in committing evil.

Azazel was not the only teacher. Semyaza and other angels also tutored the humans on how to survive on earth.

Unwilling to put up with this activity, God sent the angel Raphael to lead a heavenly army to earth. Naturally they were victorious, and they told Semyaza, leader of the Watchers, God's decree for him. His violent sons would destroy one another (using the weapons Azazel taught them to make), then Semyaza and his allies would be bound until a judgment day when they will be sent "to the abyss of fire; in torment and in prison they will be shut up for all eternity" (*1 Enoch* 10:19). Good angels will battle evil ones and triumph, and there will be a judgment day, the evil angels will be imprisoned in fire and suffer for all eternity—all future basics of the Christian belief about devils. Somewhat superfluously, Enoch brought the message about all this to Azazel.

First Enoch repeats this theme a number of times, emphasizing its prominence, but other themes appear, such as the names of the angels who guarded the Garden of Eden to keep Adam and Eve from returning. The chief guardian is Gabriel, who is helped by Uriel.

The book takes another important step, identifying the gods of the pagans as demons, something the Christians would later accept as standard.

This notion was much debated in the ancient world. Many people thought the pagan gods simply did not exist. The book of Isaiah (chapter 44) presents a caustic picture of a pagan workman taking a piece of wood and carving it into a god that he then worships—venerating a god that he made himself! The workman used the leftover wood to cook his lunch, and the biblical writer leaves no doubt that the workman made better use of the wood that way than in making an idol.

But sometimes the pagan gods seemed to have power. Moses and his brother Aaron engaged in a contest of power with two magicians of Pharaoh. They turned their staffs into serpents, and then Moses turned Aaron's staff into one powerful serpent that promptly swallowed the other two (Exod 7:8-13). Moses triumphed, but Pharaoh's magicians still had the power to turn their staffs into serpents.

First Enoch accepts that the gods have power but then gave the "gods" a transforming interpretation. They are not deities but demons (19:3). This would become a standard Christian explanation of any power apparently demonstrated by the pagan gods.

Although Azazel and Semyaza occupy prominent places among the evil angels, *1 Enoch* does refer to Satan (53:3), not as an evil being, but as one carrying out the commands of God to punish evildoers—the traditional biblical view of Satan as adversary—yet it also refers to the servants of Satan as evil (54:6). The picture of the evil one was still taking shape.

Collecting traditions left and right, *1 Enoch* says that angels brought about the Great Flood, thus not having God do the deed directly, while an evil angel named Gadreel, a follower of Semyaza, leads Eve astray in the Garden of Eden—an identification not found anywhere else in Jewish literature but also an assertion that an evil, fallen angel had deceived Eve.

Turning from demons to angels, *1 Enoch* identifies Uriel, not Michael, as the leader of the heavenly host (74:1). This is a minor point, but it demonstrates the fluidity of Jewish apocryphal traditions since Michael would return as the angels' leader in the book of Revelation.

This wide-ranging book also includes some minor legendary facts—for example, that Eden was not flooded during the Noachic Flood.

The wandering, inclusive, and allusive *1 Enoch* had great authority for Jews but also for Christians, and not just the author of the book of Jude. Several Christian authors saw allusions to Jesus in *1 Enoch*, which enhanced its influence. More important was its influence on the image of the devil. Even though it does not offer a consistent diabology, it does contain much material that Christians would use to create their notion of the devil.

The Book of Jubilees was probably written about the same time as *1 Enoch*; where it was written remains uncertain. As the title suggests, it deals much with feast days and festivals.

Unlike the Old Testament writers, the author of *Jubilees* took the Garden of Eden very seriously. He basically followed the Genesis account but added details, such as that Adam and Eve lived in the Garden of Eden for seven years before the Fall. The book also mentions what became a staple of legend: before the Fall the animals in Eden could speak (*Jubilees* 3:28). This legend reached Christians in the Middle Ages when the belief arose that at midnight on Christmas Eve at the birth of Jesus—the New Adam according to the apostle Paul (Rom 5:12-14)—the animals could speak again for a few minutes because Jesus had come to make up for the sin of the first Adam. For the record, the language spoken in Eden was Hebrew (*Jubilees* 12:26).

The Watcher Angels appear, reappear, and once again have relations with human women who give birth to giants. Expanding upon opening chapters of Genesis, *Jubilees* goes to the Great Flood, after which Noah warns his children about evil angels, wicked spirits who will try to corrupt them, and then asks God for help. God sends his angels to bind the wicked demons, but their leader, here called Mastema, asks God not to send all of them to perdition. With no explanation, God

agrees and allows one-tenth of Mastema's followers to
remain on earth. This is probably a way to explain how
evil remained on earth after the Flood. It also repeats
the notion of an angelic fall from heaven and divine
punishment for them. Etymologically the names "Mastema" and "Satan" are linked, although *Jubilees* always
distinguishes the two. Also, *Jubilees* occasionally uses
the title Beliar, but Mastema is definitely the preferred
name for the leader of the demons.

Mastema certainly made use of the opportunity God
gave him. *Jubilees* tells us that his angels egged humans
on to "every kind of sin and uncleanness" (*Jubilees* 11)
but especially idolatry, the most serious sin in the Old
Testament. Perhaps knowing that God would work
through Abraham, Mastema petulantly sent ravens to
ruin the crops of Abraham's father Terah.

One of the more barbaric biblical accounts is that of
God's asking Abraham to sacrifice his only son Isaac as
proof of his devotion. Why would God ask a human sacrifice of his chosen one, Abraham? Could not an omni-
scient being *know* that Abraham was loyal? The author
of *Jubilees* turns this account into a parody of the book
of Job.

He says that the "prince" Mastema comes into God's
presence and challenges God to prove that Abraham is
faithful to him by asking for the sacrifice of Isaac. The author emphasizes that "the Lord knew that Abraham was
faithful" (*Jubilees* 17), but God still agreed to the request.
Abraham obeys God who prevents the sacrifice at the last
moment. *Jubilees* adds that Mastema was present at this
event and that "prince Mastema was put to shame."

Note the similarities to Satan in Job: Mastema is in
the presence of God, not in hell, nor does God expel
him from heaven or order him to leave. When Mastema
makes his outrageous proposal, God goes along with it.
Here Mastema acts like an adversary, and while he was

put to shame, there is no hint that he has here done anything morally wrong (in this particular event).

In the book of Exodus, God calls Moses to return to Egypt and free the Hebrews from slavery. Moses agrees and sets off, but, for no clear reason, God attempts to kill Moses along the way (Exod 4:24). Jewish and Christian scholars have been trying to make sense out of this difficult passage for 2500 years. But the author of *Jubilees* solved the problem in his own way: Mastema, not God, tried to kill Moses (*Jubilees* 48). When that did not work, Mastema went to Egypt to help the sorcerers in their test of strength against Moses, then he killed all the firstborn of Egypt (the tenth plague), topping it all off by encouraging the Egyptians to pursue the fleeing Hebrews!

Just as the Old Testament writers used Satan to do some of God's rather questionable work, so does the author of *Jubilees* do with Mastema. Evil as he might be, Mastema has not been separated completely from God's activity.

Another Jewish work, contemporary with Jesus himself, was *The Life of Adam and Eve*, but early versions of this work do not survive, and many surviving manuscripts have what appear to be Christian additions.

The book recounts what happened to the primal couple after their expulsion from the Garden of Eden. Here the serpent in the Garden is explicitly identified as the devil, but more details appear. The devil continues to persecute Adam and Eve even after their expulsion, and so Adam asks the devil why he does that. The devil replies that he had been the leader of many of the angels in heaven when God announced that he had created Adam in his image and likeness. This made Adam superior to the angels, whom God commanded to venerate Adam and sent the angel Michael to make sure that all of them did. The devil and those angels who followed him refused to worship Adam, and so God expelled them from heaven. The devil got his revenge against God by tempting Adam and Eve to sin.

The book goes on to say that Satan is leader of some angels, and Michael leads them all, but there is no mention of a war in heaven between angelic groups. God simply uses his own power to expel those who would not venerate Adam.

Another Jewish work, written about the same time, was *The Assumption of Moses*, which provides more details on the actual temptation in the Garden. Both books make it clear that Satan tempted the primal couple in the form of a serpent.

The book of the Wisdom of Solomon, accepted as biblical by Roman Catholics and Orthodox but rejected by Protestants and Jews, has a single sentence that probably reflects this Jewish view: "Through the devil's envy death entered the world" (2:24).

The last Jewish apocryphon to consider is the *Testaments of the Twelve Patriarchs*, written in Hebrew or Aramaic in Judea in the first century BC or AD. It purports to be the final testaments of the twelve sons of Jacob. Throughout the *Testaments* the evil spirit is Beliar, who appears in the New Testament as Belial (2 Cor 6:15). The "testaments" wander all over the place, alighting upon random subjects. Beliar acts like the traditional villain, leading other spirits in a constant campaign against humans, and he is compared to the Lord as darkness to light. But there is a new note here.

One of the twelve patriarchs, Reuben, is a blatant misogynist: "Women are evil, my children. . . . they use wiles and try to subdue him [the man] by their charms. . . . command your wives and daughters not to adorn their heads and faces, for every woman that uses wiles of this kind has been reserved for eternal punishment. It was thus they *allured the Watchers* before the Flood" (Test. Reuben 5). Note the sexist change: women used makeup to allure the Watchers, whereas the previous tradition in *1 Enoch* was that the Watchers taught women how to use makeup.

There is more: "The Watchers . . . conceived the act in their minds and changed themselves into the shape of men and appeared to the women when they were having intercourse with their husbands. And the women, lusting in their minds after the phantom forms, gave birth to giants" (*Test. Reuben* 5). This is an early appearance of a traditional demonic notion, the *incubus*, an evil spirit who takes the shape of a man to seduce a woman. (A *succubus* is a demon who takes the form of a woman to seduce a man.)

Although not generally well known, the Jewish apocrypha played a decisive role in what would become the Christian notion of the devil. Jesus, his first disciples, and most writers of the New Testament were Jews to whom this literature or at least the notions contained in it would have been familiar.

We should also remember that the canon, the list of inspired books, of the Hebrew Bible had not been finalized at the time these books were composed, nor at the time when Jesus was teaching, nor when the earliest New Testament books were being composed. The traditional date for setting the canon is AD 90 when a group of rabbis in Palestine met in a town called Jamnia to decide on which books they considered inspired. Unfortunately, the evidence for this meeting is not strong, and the setting of the canon may have occurred later. But this means that when the apocryphal books were composed, they were not "apocryphal" because the canon had not been established, and these books had more authority than they would have after being designated noncanonical.

For generations scholars relied upon the Old Testament and Jewish tradition to delineate and understand Jewish views on many matters, not just Satan. But in the mid-twentieth century, thanks to a trove of manuscripts discovered in caves near Qumran on the northwest shore of the Dead Sea—the famous Dead Sea Scrolls—scholars learned of a previously unknown Jewish sect that, in the second century BC, had withdrawn from mainstream Jewish life to live in a sectarian community, which lasted until the Romans destroyed it during the Romano-Jewish War of AD 66–70. Many scholars think these Jews were the Essenes, a group referred to in several sources but whose identifiable works have not survived.

Essenes or not, the Qumran Jews were contemporaries of the Maccabean kings of Judea, of Herod, of Pilate, and also of Jesus and his disciples. Study of the scrolls has provided some valuable information about the world of the New Testament.

But do the scrolls say anything about the devil? Yes, but not much.

Several scrolls refer to *satan* not as a proper noun but rather as the word for "adversary." H. A. Kelly (*Satan: A Biography*, 44) points out that the scrolls refer to *mastema* but, like *satan*, as a common noun, in this case meaning "adversary." But one proper name does appear.

The Qumran Jews had apocalyptic notions that they put into practice by joining the Jewish revolt against Roman rule. One scroll is vigorously titled *The War of the Sons of Light against the Son of Darkness*, marking a strict dichotomy between good and evil. The Qumran Jews may have fought on earth, but "war" took place throughout the cosmos, and the leader of the Sons of Darkness was Belial. That the evil leader had this name shows how fluid and uncertain was the name of the evil spirits' leader since we have already seen him referred to as Mastema, Semyaza, Azazel, and, of course, Satan.

Unfortunately the Qumran Jews used Belial in another context. Naturally they had no use for the unclean Gentiles, but they considered themselves the only pure Jews, and so all other Jews, who did not keep the word of God as they did, were not really followers of God but of Belial. The Qumran Jews did what no one had done before, accusing fellow believers of being in league with evil spirits, a practice with a long history among Christians who routinely demonized heretics in the Middle Ages and which became something of a perverted art form in the Catholic-Protestant polemics during the sixteenth-century Reformation.

But, helpful as they may be to New Testament scholars, the Qumran Jews did not represent the future. Indeed, as a community, they simply disappeared after the Roman attack of AD 68. The future of Judaism lay with a very different group: the rabbis.

The Roman-Jewish war of 66–70 ended in the destruction of the temple in Jerusalem and much else in Jewish society. A group we now recognize as the rabbis worked to keep the Palestinian Jews together and to make religion a force in their lives. The rabbis mostly believed in demons, whose numbers were endless and who resembled angels, that is, supernatural beings with wings. But the rabbis generally relegated the demons to folklore; like Lilith, they lived in desolate places, they ate, drank, and reproduced themselves. Their chief negative impact on humans was causing illnesses. Prayers could keep them at bay; sometimes special amulets could do so as well.

The rabbis accepted the absolute oneness and sovereignty of God (Deut 4:35), and, so they could not extend to demons the power of causing people to do evil. They concluded that all humans have within them two inclinations, one to good and the other to evil, but they also have free will and, with God's aid, can overcome the evil inclinations.

Rabbinic views on evil require far more explanation, but, most important for us, they did not see Satan as a major element in human evil, and they certainly did not see him as the Christians did, a formidable evil being who was for some reason permitted by God to carry out depredations upon human bodies and spirits.

The devil so familiar to Christian believers has a background—as do all Christian beliefs and teachings—in the Old Testament and in Jewish culture, but only a background. The devil is simply not an Old Testament figure, but one who emerges from the pages of the New Testament, to which we will now turn.

CHAPTER FOUR

The Devil
in the New Testament
The Pauline Epistles

The New Testament is the name given by the Christian church to a collection of twenty-seven diverse
books that emerged from the first century of the
church's history and that Christians believe to have
been inspired by God, just as the books of the Old
Testament were.

But inspiration does not obviate complication, and
the New Testament books can be very complex.

The natural assumption that believers would make is
that the New Testament books started chronologically
with the gospels, the first books in printed New Testaments, because these are biographies of Jesus, two of
which were written by members of the twelve apostles.
The New Testament then goes on to the epistles of the
apostle Paul, the later epistles which were composed
by Jesus' immediate disciples, an early church history
titled the Acts of the Apostles, and ending appropriately
enough with the book of Revelation or Apocalypse written by the apostle John. In fact, the situation is quite
different.

Nineteenth-century biblical scholars demonstrated that the gospels are not biographies but "kerygmas" (preachings), heavily theological accounts of Jesus' public ministry, suffering, death, and resurrection. They cannot be biographies because they say almost nothing of his life before his public ministry. The gospels of Matthew and Luke recount his birth, and Luke tells of an event when Jesus was twelve, but none provides any information beyond that.

Modern scholars also demonstrated that Matthew and John could not be members of the twelve apostles, a phrase that only appears once in the gospels, Matthew 10:2, although Luke 6:13 speaks of "twelve, whom he named apostles." Otherwise the evangelists—that is, the gospel writers—just use the phrase "the Twelve." Literary analysis and comparison of Mark and Matthew's gospels shows that Matthew was dependent upon Mark, who was not one of the Twelve and never even knew the historical Jesus. Why would an eyewitness to the career of Jesus depend upon an account by someone who was not?

What about John, "the disciple whom Jesus loved" (John 13:23)? Scholars point out that nowhere in this gospel is the Beloved Disciple identified as John. Further, as we shall see, this gospel has a very advanced theology of Christ, one demonstrating a sophisticated, educated, fluently Greek author who could not have been a Galilean fisherman.

Since Mark and Luke were not members of the twelve apostles, this means that none of the evangelists were witnesses to the events of Jesus' life. This may sound a bit surprising, but it is the view of Orthodox, Roman Catholic, and mainline Protestant biblical scholars.

Scholars also determined that Mark wrote about the year 70, Matthew and Luke in the 80s, and John about

the year 100. All wrote in Greek for Christian communities in the central and eastern Mediterranean lands.
Since Greek was not the language of Jesus, this means
that we do not have Jesus' original words in Aramaic,
except for the occasional phrase.

This does not mean that we do not have reliable evidence about Jesus' public ministry, but it does mean that
we must accept that the evangelists wrote for Christians
of their own day and adapted their material for their con-
gregations, much the way contemporary preachers use
examples from and references to modern life. This also
means that the gospel picture of Satan originated with
Jesus who proclaimed it in Galilee in a language called
Aramaic but was preserved by Greek-speaking, educated
people who never met Jesus. This also means that the
biblical writers who tell us about him may have developed his teaching in the period between his death and
the writing of a particular biblical book.

The dates of the gospels also impact how we understand the New Testament teaching about Satan. The
earliest gospel written was that of Mark about the year
70. Since the apostle Paul was executed in Rome around
the year 64, this means that all of his epistles predate
even the earliest gospel. So the earliest Christian images
of the devil emerge from Paul's epistles and thus from
his understanding of what Jesus taught and not directly
from Jesus' own teaching. Of course, we have strong
reason to believe that Paul, who died for his faith, had
every intention of being faithful to Jesus' teaching on all
matters.

But Paul lived in a different world from the limited
one experienced by Jesus. He was a diasporan Jew from
the city of Tarsus in southeastern Asia Minor, probably born around the same time as Jesus. He grew up in
a Greek-speaking environment. He was a tentmaker,
which was most likely his family's profession. He was

a Roman citizen, and he received rabbinic training in Jerusalem. Religiously, he belonged to the Pharisees, the group in the gospels who often opposed Jesus but also a devout lay brotherhood who put much emphasis on education. Around the year 35 he converted to Christianity, after first having been a persecutor! Once he gained the trust of the disciples in the Jerusalem community, Paul embarked on a career as a missionary, mostly among the Gentiles of the Eastern Mediterranean and Greece. He also wrote a number of epistles, seven of which survive, six to these communities and one personal letter. He also wrote letters that are not extant.

Paul became the major figure in the expansion of Christianity into Gentile areas. When he returned to Judea about the year 62, his Jewish enemies brought charges against him, portraying him to the Roman governor as a disturber of the peace and thus a threat to the government. As a Roman citizen, Paul had the right to have his case heard in Rome. He exercised that right and went to Rome, where he was executed. Scholars do not know if that was because he lost his case and suffered capital punishment or whether he died in Nero's persecution of the Christians in 64.

Libraries have been written about Paul, but let us highlight just three of his greatest achievements.

- He knew only the risen Christ, and he single-handedly broke a pending monopoly about the understanding of Jesus by those who knew him. If preaching and teaching and writing about Jesus depended upon knowledge of the historical person, Christianity would have died out in a few decades. Paul made Christianity possible by his emphasis on the importance of the risen Christ who is still present to the community.

- He brought the gospel message to Gentiles at a time when many disciples, including Peter, leader of the Twelve, and James, head of the Jerusalem community and a relative of Jesus, anticipated a mission only to Jews. Modern worldwide Christianity has its foundation in his missionizing.

- He produced the oldest extant Christian literature, his seven authentic epistles: 1 Thessalonians, 1–2 Corinthians, Romans, Galatians, Philippians, and Philemon. Although often written in response to immediate situations, these epistles also contain the earliest account of Christian teaching as well as the earliest Christian theology, especially Christology, the theology of Christ. Twenty centuries later Paul still influences Christian belief and teaching, including that on the devil.

So what did the first Christian writer say about this evil figure?

For starters, he never used the word *diábolos* but did use Satan as a proper noun seven times (Rom 16:20; 1 Cor 5:5; 7:5; 2 Cor 2:11; 11:14; 12:7; 1 Thess 2:18). He also referred to Belial once (2 Cor 6:15). He used the word "demon" four times but in just two consecutive sentences (1 Cor 10:20-21) when he contrasted allegiance to Christ with allegiance to false gods and demons, and he equated the two. Thus for Paul, the evil spirit, the enemy of Christians, was named Satan.

Paul was a well-educated diasporan Jew, and so we should expect that his views on many religious matters would draw upon the Hebrew Bible, some of the Jewish Apocrypha, and contemporary Jewish religious tradition, especially that of the Pharisees.

Paul's earliest letter, 1 Thessalonians, written about AD 49, was to the community at Thessalonica, a city in Macedonia where he had preached and founded a church. The Thessalonians, like most early Christians, believed in the imminent end of the age, a view Paul shared and which was usually called the *Parousia*. Beyond that, they expected to be alive when it happened, and they became puzzled when some members of the community died. Paul wrote to deal with this problem and with some lesser matters.

He had to write rather than visit because he "wanted again and again [to join them]—but Satan blocked our way" (1 Thess 2:18). In his earliest New Testament appearance, Satan is doing what he will always do: try to find a way to thwart Jesus' message from reaching people.

A few years later Paul wrote to a community in Corinth, a city in mainland Greece. He had founded the church there around 52, but by about 55 he had learned of serious factionalism there that split Christian against Christian. He wrote 1 Corinthians to address the factionalism and then went on to discuss many other issues in this second longest of his letters. He made two direct references to Satan.

The first reference concerns a man who committed incest. Paul advised his readers to "hand this man over to Satan for the destruction of the flesh, so that his spirit may be saved in the day of the Lord" (1 Cor 5:5). Here Satan has charge of physical punishment of sinners but for a good purpose since the man might achieve salvation on the Day of the Lord—that is, when Jesus returns to judge the living and the dead.

This passage has a similarity to the book of Job. Satan is not evil but is punishing an evildoer who was "handed over" to him, the same phrase God said to Satan in Job 2:6: "Behold, I am handing him over to you" (my translation), but Satan cannot take Job's life. This verse implies that Satan does not always act in an evil way; here he carries out Paul's will for the sinful man.

Further along in the epistle (7:5) Paul warned the Corinthians that Satan could take advantage of them when they lose their self-control, here referring to sexual desire. Satan has again become threatening, a tempter, because if people lose control he "will put you to the test." Alluding to the sins of the Israelites in the desert during the Exodus, he also told the Corinthians "not [to] put Christ to the test" because when the Israelites put God to the test, "they were destroyed by the destroyer" (10:10), apparently a reference to Satan because once again people are destroyed physically but not spiritually.

Shortly after writing 1 Corinthians Paul wrote a brief epistle that would later be combined with another one to form what is now 2 Corinthians. This composite letter includes three references to Satan, two of which allude to his deviousness. Paul first spoke of punishing a sinner but then forgiving him "so that we may not be outwitted by Satan; for we are not ignorant of his designs" (2 Cor 2:11). This relates to the passages in 1 Corinthians—secular punishment but not loss of the person spiritually.

At 2 Corinthians 11:14 Paul makes a famous reference. Some other Christian missionaries had challenged Paul's work and even his person, so Paul struck back fiercely: "For such boasters are false apostles, deceitful workers, disguising themselves as apostles of Christ. And no wonder! Even Satan disguises himself as an angel of light."

Again Paul warned of Satan's deviousness and linked him with the angels, and, like the Jews at Qumran, Paul saw other believers who disagreed with him as being in league with Satan. Furthermore, the reference to an angel of light is borrowed from Qumran or at least from some intermediary who knew Qumran teachings since these referred to an angel of light to combat the prince of darkness.

(Let us note that these other, so-called "false" apostles whom Paul loathed were also devoting themselves to Christ's work and even risking their lives for it. Since they disagreed with Paul, they have historically been treated negatively, but we know from Paul himself (Gal 2:11-14) that Peter, head of the Twelve, and James, head of the Jerusalem community, also disagreed with him.)

Paul's next reference to Satan suggests continued Old Testament influence. He told the Corinthians that "to keep me from being too elated, a thorn was given me" (12:7) by Satan's angel. To his credit, Paul acknowledged that he did not want this correction and prayed to the Lord three times for it to be removed, only to be told, "My grace is enough for you." Paul was getting elated, the Lord wished to save him from that, and so he employed Satan to find a way to bring Paul back—very much the Satan of the Old Testament.

At the end of his last (AD 58) and longest letter, to the Romans, Paul assured his correspondents that "The God of peace will shortly crush Satan under your feet" (16:20). Many exegetes and preachers align this with God's words to the Eden serpent (Gen 3:15) that the serpent will strike at the woman's offspring's heel while he will strike at the serpent's head, a reference Christians traditionally applied to Mary and Jesus. But, as Henry Kelly notes (*The Devil at Baptism*, 63–64), Genesis speaks of ongoing enmity while Romans speaks of a total defeat of Satan. In Romans, Paul is basically presenting Satan as an enemy of Christians but one whom God will fully overcome.

And what about the reference to Belial—the only one in the New Testament? It appears in 2 Corinthians: "What has Christ to do with Belial?" (6:15; my translation). This question is part of a paragraph in which Paul warned Christians about getting too close to unbelievers and to stay away from pagan temples and their false deities. He used the image of Belial to personify these threats rather than the daily tempter Satan.

But Paul had more to say about Satan than just these direct references.

As we have seen, the writers of the Old Testament had little interest in Adam and Eve. The authors of the Jewish apocryphal literature had more interest but never raised the Garden of Eden to cosmic status. Yet Paul identifies Jesus as the New Adam who came to redeem the world from the consequences of the first Adam's sin. He also spoke about the Garden: "But I am afraid that as the serpent deceived Eve by its cunning, your thoughts will be led astray from a sincere and pure devotion to Christ" (2 Cor 11:3). There he mentioned Eve more than the entire the Hebrew Bible does outside of Genesis 2–3, but he does not pursue the topic. Nor does he identify the serpent with Satan, but this passage does come right before his warning that Satan could disguise himself as an angel of light. Did Paul mean to imply that Satan had also disguised himself as a serpent? But why not just make the identification?

Paul's use of Adam did not make Adam a major figure. Only two other New Testament writers refer to Adam, the pseudonymous epistle of Jude who just mentions his name (v. 14) and the equally pseudonymous author of 1 Timothy who cites the Eden account to show the trouble that women can cause and thus to justify restricting their role in the church.

Paul himself left another vague reference in 1 Corinthians 11:10. Trying to find a justification for requiring women to wear veils to cover their hair, he gave several reasons why this was the natural thing to do, and then added "because of the angels." This might refer to a Jewish, especially Qumran, belief that angels were guardians of the natural order of propriety, but it also might refer to the Watcher Angels who, according to the misogynistic author of *1 Enoch*, were lured from heaven by the beauty of women.

Did Paul say anything about hell? He said that Christ has conquered death (1 Cor 15:26); and very famously, "Where, O Death, is your sting?" (14:55). He made it clear that the good would receive blessedness, but he never really specified what postmortem punishment (if any) there would be for the wicked. He referred to death as the last enemy (15:26) and makes it clear that those who are resurrected from death belong to Christ (15:24). He asked, "Do you not know that the wrong-doers will not inherit the kingdom of God?" (6:9). He speaks of judgment and of how God will judge the good and wicked but does not say what will happen to the wicked subsequent to that judgment. He warns that evil-doers will experience "wrath and fury. . . . anguish and distress" (Rom 2:8-9), but further along in that epistle (11:32) he expresses his hope that God will have mercy on all.

Paul never denied the existence of postmortem punishment or of hell, but he never explicitly mentioned either of them. He may have believed in extinction, that is, those who cannot enter the joy of the Lord simply cease to exist. Obviously, the fate of the good and the evil is a mystery, and Paul could not pronounce finally on it, but since he grew up in Asia Minor, a heavily Gentile environment where belief in postmortem punishment was common, and since he would have been familiar with Jewish apocryphal works that certainly did speak of postmortem punishment, his reticence on this issue is surprising.

CHAPTER FIVE

The Devil in the Gospels
Mark and Matthew

The apostle Paul pioneered many things, including Christology, the theology of Christ, and the idea of the New Adam. But Paul's letters had diverse focuses, and he never produced a full Christology. In contrast, the evangelists—the gospel writers—focused their entire writings on Jesus, and each of the four produced a Christology. This means that the gospels are primarily theological documents, but ones that contain much biographical information.

This presents a problem for many believers who were brought up to think of the gospels as biographies of Jesus. Certainly the gospels are not biographies as moderns understand the term. Only two (Matthew and Luke) mention Jesus' birth, and Luke provides the only account of him between his birth and public career that Luke said began when he was "about thirty" (3:23). Biographical information about Jesus was incorporated into the gospel Christologies.

Are there any specific dates? Not really. Luke tells us that Jesus was born during the reign of the Roman emperor Caesar Augustus, but that ran from 31 BC to AD 14. His public career occurred during the governorship of Pontius Pilate, which went from 26 to AD 36. Jesus was born during the reign of the Roman-appointed Jewish king Herod, but that was from 37 to 4 BC.

(Obvious question: if Jesus was born during Herod's reign, which ended in 4 BC, how can Christ be born "Before Christ"? In the sixth century a Syrian monk named Dionysius Exiguus prepared the BC/AD calendar, and he miscalculated the dates of Herod's reign. Later scholars realized his mistake and corrected it.)

But that does not mean that we know nothing about Jesus' life. On the contrary, we know quite a bit. While we cannot say that he taught the parable of the Good Samaritan on September 27 in the year AD 32, we do have an outline of his life.

- He was a Jew
- His parents were Miriam (Mary) and Joseph, who was a carpenter
- He was born in the Judean town of Bethlehem during the reign of the Roman-appointed Jewish king Herod
- He was raised in Nazareth in Galilee
- He could read (Luke 4:17) and write (John 8:6)
- He followed his father's profession, a standard practice in the ancient world
- He began his public career shortly after that of the charismatic prophet John the Baptist
- He gathered disciples of both sexes and chose twelve men to be special disciples who were later called the twelve apostles
- He preached and worked mostly in small towns in Galilee

- He was well versed in Jewish traditions and could debate biblical passages with members of the Pharisees, a pious, Jewish lay brotherhood
- He traveled about the countryside
- He could relate to people of all classes from peasants to the wealthy
- His mission provoked opposition from some Jewish groups, especially the Pharisees
- He traveled to Jerusalem where the common people welcomed him while the local authorities feared his influence and his threat to their status as official leaders of the people
- The Jerusalem authorities engineered his trial and conviction as a dangerous troublemaker
- The Roman governor Pontius Pilate ordered his execution by crucifixion
- He died and rose from the dead

Although this is not enough material to write a modern biography, the gospels do provide a good deal of information about Jesus' earthly life. But we must also bear in mind that the evangelists were writing for other Christians—that is, they did not try to prove that Jesus was the Son of God or the Redeemer or the Messiah. They were explaining who Jesus was and is to those who already believed in him. This can be seen in the opening passage of the oldest gospel, Mark: "The beginning of the good news [Gospel] of Jesus Christ, the Son of God" (1:1). Mark just proclaims it and does not try to prove it because his readers already believed in Jesus.

The New Testament approach mirrors that of the Old Testament, whose first verses say, "In the beginning God created the heavens and the earth"—no attempt at proof for the existence of God, just a statement of belief by one Jew to other Jews.

Much gospel Christology deals with Jesus and the devil.

Mark

Mark wrote his gospel around the year 70. He did not explain why he wrote an account of Jesus when oral tradition had served the community so well for three decades. Since Peter, Paul, James, and other Christian leaders, as well as many Christians who had known Jesus personally, had died, Mark may have feared that valuable traditions about Jesus could possibly be lost. Mark may also have concluded that a written account was necessary to preserve those traditions. Mark was a converted Jew who lived in the Diaspora, probably in the eastern Mediterranean but possibly in Rome. He would have been familiar with the Old Testament and Jewish literature.

The devil makes an immediate appearance in the gospel (1:12) after Jesus' baptism by John at the River Jordan: "He was in the wilderness forty days, tempted by Satan." Mark does not make it clear if this is a negative act on Satan's part or if he is still acting like an Old Testament figure, sent by God to test someone. But Jesus passes the test and begins his career.

Now Mark turns to his real interest—demonic possession. He recounts that Jesus drove out an "unclean spirit" from a man (1:23-26) and goes on to add "all who were sick or possessed with demons" (1:32), indicating a sizeable number of possessed people. When Paul spoke of demons, he meant the pagan gods, whom he did not take seriously, following the prophet Isaiah (44:13-17) for whom these deities were created by humans. But Mark speaks very differently of demons. First, he is writing about Jews, not Gentiles, and Jews did not venerate demons—that is, the demons in this gospel differ considerably from those Paul wrote about. Second, these demons not only exist but are dangerous.

Mark does speak of Satan but only a half-dozen times and three of those times in a space of four verses (3:23-26), and he never uses the word "devil." He makes one reference to Beelzebul (3:22) where he calls him "the prince of demons." The evangelists Luke and Matthew would follow Mark on this point, using "demon" more frequently than "devil" and occasionally identifying the two. This practice has maintained itself for two millennia; for example, the study of the devil is traditionally called demonology, not diabology.

The demons would work against Jesus, but Mark introduced an important new note: the demons possess people, and Jesus drives them out of the possessed in a process called exorcism. The gospels portray Jesus as a great exorcist, engaging in a contest of power against evil spirits. The notion of exorcism was not new; there were Jewish exorcists (Matt 12:27; Acts 19:13). But for Mark, Matthew, and Luke, exorcism became a central concern of Jesus' mission.

The exorcist strives to free a person from demonic possession, but what exactly is demonic possession? Different churches define it in different ways, but in the Bible possession means that an evil spirit has taken control of the person's body and forced her or him to perform acts that others would find repugnant, such as running about naked (Luke 8:27), groveling on the ground (Mark 9:17-18), or demonstrating almost superhuman strength (Mark 5:4). No doubt ancient people ascribed demonic possession to phenomena we would recognize today as physical, mental, or emotional illness. Yet even allowing for that, the gospels present demonic possession as a real and potent challenge to Jesus' mission.

But a problem arises. Since Christians believe that people possessed by an evil spirit cannot be held guilty for what they do under possession (that is, they cannot sin), why would an evil spirit want to possess someone since ultimately no harm comes to that person? The New Testament never says, but the answer probably lies in Genesis 1:26, where God creates humans in his image and likeness. Someone lying in muck and growling like a beast no longer—on the surface at least—reflects the image of God. Possession denies the very basics of what it means to be human and, as such, challenges God and his authority over the world.

Mark makes possession sound common: "That evening, at sunset, they [the people of Capernaum] brought to him *all* who were sick or *possessed with demons*. . . . He cured many who were sick with various diseases, and *cast out many demons*" (Mark 1:32-34). And this was a small town. Since Mark says those who were ill also came, it may be that the local people attributed a variety of illnesses to evil spirits. It is also noteworthy that every reference Mark makes to a demon involves possession.

The possession accounts also show a different development. "And the scribes who came down from Jerusalem said, 'He [Jesus] has Beelzebul, and by the ruler of the demons he casts out demons'" (Mark 3:22). Mark here associates a name from the Jewish apocrypha with a word used to describe pagan idols. That term along with "Satan," "devil," and "demon" are the only words for evil spirits—that is, Mark is abandoning the multifarious and difficult-to-justify names and persons, such as Mastema and Semyaza. As Father Michael Patella puts it so directly, "In the gospels 'Satan,' 'devil,' and 'Beelzebul' are used interchangeably" (*Angels and Demons*, 171, n. 7). Mark does this and also drops the distinction between demons and evil spirits. All the diverse evil beings of the Jewish apocrypha are being banded together as supernatural enemies of Jesus.

Mark does something else, identifying Beelzebul (a word he uses only once) as the prince of demons—that is, the evil horde has a leader.

Matthew and Luke, who used Mark's gospel as the base for theirs, used the word Beelzebul three times each, and five of those six usages are in their versions of Mark's account of the accusation that Jesus had aligned himself with Beelzebul (Matt 12:24-27; Luke 11:15-19). They did, however, change those who challenged Jesus from Jerusalem scribes to Pharisees (Matthew) or just people in the crowd (Luke). Both of the other evangelists also referred to Beelzebul as the prince of demons, thus accepting Mark's contention that the evil spirits have a leader, although otherwise they dropped the name "Beelzebul" and generally referred to him as "Satan."

After Mark

For whatever reason Mark wrote his gospel, it was a success that inspired other Christian authors. A dozen or so years after the first gospel came the next two, written at approximately the same time in the 80s. Like Mark, Matthew was apparently a diasporan Jew who, in his gospel, worked hard to demonstrate that Jesus the Messiah was indeed the one promised by the prophets, even if he suffered and died to save his people rather than coming down from heaven with an angelic army to drive the Romans into the sea. Many of Matthew's readers would have been converted Jews.

Luke was a Gentile, probably the only Gentile to write a New Testament book. Throughout his gospel he portrays Jesus as the universal savior who came from God to save humankind from its sins. Many examples from the gospels can demonstrate these concerns, but here is just one. Both evangelists provide a genealogy for Jesus, but Matthew (1:1-17) traces Jesus' ancestry back

to Abraham, father of the Jewish people, while Luke
(3:23-38) traces it back to Adam, father of the entire
human race.

But their views on the devil are quite similar. Luke
also wrote a second book, the Acts of the Apostles, that
traces the growth of the church under the guidance of
the Holy Spirit into Gentile lands, and he speaks of the
devil in that book, too.

Both evangelists had Mark's gospel in front of them,
and they generally followed his outline but added significant amounts of material, such as the infancy narratives (Matthew 1–2, Luke 1–2) and many sayings and
parallels. They also expanded upon Mark's teaching
about evil spirits.

Matthew

Although considerably longer than Mark, Matthew
does not have many more references to Satan and the
devil, making a half dozen references to each, but eight
of those twelve combined references appear in just two
chapters (4 and 12). Matthew also makes a dozen references to demons, all in relation to exorcism. He thus
separates the demons from Satan/devil. Dangerous as
demons may be, they work on a low level, plaguing individual human beings. Satan/devil, on the other hand,
chooses a more formidable target.

Mark said that Jesus spent forty days in the desert,
an obvious parallel to the Hebrews' forty years in the
Exodus and quite possibly a parallel created by Jesus
himself. Matthew repeats that but goes well beyond
Mark, recounting a give-and-take conversation between
Jesus and Satan, identified as the Tester or Tempter or
as the devil (4:1-11).

What follows resembles a dispute between two rabbis
as Satan and Jesus debate via citations of Scriptural

passages. Satan's first temptation is intended to see if Jesus is indeed the Son of God by having him demonstrate his divine sonship by performing a "simple" miracle: turning stones into bread. Jesus refuses to do so but rather quotes Deuteronomy 8:3 in reply.

Not stymied for long, Satan brings Jesus to the parapet of the Jerusalem temple (presumably via a vision since they remain in the desert) and urges him to throw himself down as no harm would come to the Son of God because angels would rescue him. Satan then cites Psalm 91 in support of his challenge. Jesus again resorts to Deuteronomy (6:16) for a telling response.

Finally the devil takes Jesus to the top of a high mountain (again via a vision) and shows him "all the kingdoms of the world in their magnificence" (4:9) and offers them to Jesus if he will prostrate himself and worship Satan. Jesus can thus be lord of the world if he gives in. Jesus again refuses, citing Deuteronomy (6:3) for the third time. Having been bested in the debate, the devil departs.

Jewish converts would have understood what was going on here, and especially the third temptation because several Israelite kings, such as Ahab (1 Kings 16:32), abandoned the worship of the true God and followed pagan gods in order to gain political power. All Matthew's readers would have understood the main point: Satan is an evil spirit determined to frustrate Jesus' mission to redeem humanity from sin.

Matthew repeats Mark's account of the accusation that Jesus drove out evil spirits by the power of Beelzebul (12:32), whom he mentions twice. In this account he openly identifies Satan with Beelzebul. Matthew makes one other reference to Beelzebul (10:25), an offhand one that is not followed up. Matthew is following not Paul but Mark, identifying Satan, the devil, and Beelzebul as one and the same.

Matthew also makes an infamous reference to Satan. In chapter 16 Jesus' disciple Peter, the leader of the Twelve, tries to discourage Jesus from a path that would lead to his death. Jesus fiercely rebukes him and actually calls him "Satan" (16:23). Of course, Peter was not really doing anything evil. Jesus had concluded that his mission would require his death, and Peter, who loved him, did not want Jesus to suffer. But Jesus saw a repetition of the temptation in the desert, someone trying to turn him from his mission.

The evangelist's final reference to Satan is a very important one. Jesus is speaking of the judgment of the nations (25:31-46), which are compared to sheep on God's right and goats on his left. Jesus' Father "will say to those at his left hand, 'You that are accursed, depart from me into the eternal fire prepared for the devil and his angels'" (Matt 25:41). Here Jesus clearly speaks of a place of eternal punishment—not a temporary one with the chance to repent—and one consisting of fire that had been "prepared for the devil and his angels," a reworking of Jewish apocryphal themes of angels who had once been blessed and who are now damned and of their leader who is there with them. Like Mark, Matthew refers to the devil as the leader of those evil beings. Yet he does not explain who the devil's angels were, that is, were they once good angels but now fallen or had they always been evil? Most Christians assume the former, but Matthew does not explain.

Matthew's main concern in this passage is the judgment of the nations, and so he leaves out some important material. For example, are Satan and his angels in this place of punishment now? Humans will join them there, but Matthew does not specify whether the devil rules over hell: that is, is he the "jailer" of the sinful humans or just one more sufferer there?

If Satan and his angels are in hell now, how are they getting out so that they can roam the earth, tempting and possessing people? Or will eternal punishment be their fate only after the day of judgment? Furthermore, this mention of the devil occurs in a passage about God judging the nations of the world. Why are they linked to the devil? Does his judgment await theirs, and, if so, why? Matthew does not explain, apparently presuming that his readers will understand.

But even with these questions remaining unanswered, Matthew has still advanced Christian demonology: the evil being challenging Jesus and his followers is Satan, also known as the devil and Beelzebul, although that second title is fading. The devil is the leader of a band of ultimately doomed evil angels who will wreak havoc in the world and also in the church—recall that Matthew was writing in the 80s when the primitive church had been established and was growing. In fact, Matthew is the only evangelist to attribute the word church, *ekklesía*, to Jesus (16:18).

CHAPTER SIX

The Devil in the Gospels
Luke, John, and Acts of the Apostles

Contemporaneously with Matthew, a Gentile convert known as Luke wrote a gospel that focused upon Jesus as the universal savior. Luke also wrote a second book called the Acts of the Apostles.

Luke probably lived in the eastern Mediterranean, possibly in the Roman province of Syria. He had a great concern for the Gentile mission but also for something else: the church.

The vast majority of Christians, including Paul (1 Thess 4:13-18), believed that the end of the age was imminent; indeed, many people looked forward to it, usually in apocalyptic terms. But by the time Luke wrote a half a century had passed since Jesus' death, and, rather disturbingly to many, the world was still here. Luke was probably not the first Christian to wonder if the end should not be expected imminently, but he was the first one to write about it. Linked to his skepticism about the end was his ecclesiology, that is, the theology of the church.

If the end was imminent, the Christians had no need for church structure and little need for new writings or particular modes of worship. They could experience the church as a group of people waiting for the end. But

Luke saw the church not just in a different light but in a much more exalted one. For him the church continued the work of the Jesus through the presence of the Holy Spirit. In all the New Testament, only Luke mentions the ascension of Jesus at the end of his gospel (24:50-52) and in the beginning of Acts (1:6-8). In the gospel Jesus advises the disciples "I am sending upon you what my Father promised; so stay here in the city until you have been clothed with power from on high" (Luke 24:49). In Acts Jesus tells the disciples (who are in Jerusalem) that "you will receive power when the Holy Spirit has come upon you" (Acts 1:8). Luke uses the same Greek word for "power" in both passages.

Luke presents Jesus leaving his disciples but also entrusting them to the Holy Spirit who will guide them. For Luke, the church, the *ekklesía* or community, continues the work of the Lord. The church is something good, something sacred, and not just a collection of people waiting for the end. This radical view challenged people and some resented it, but eventually Luke's view succeeded. Around 125, the anonymous author of the Second Epistle of Peter tried to save the notion of an imminent end (3:8-10), but the struggle had ended. Christians accepted that they would be in the world for an indefinite time; more important, they accepted that the church was indeed continuing Christ's work under the guidance of the Holy Spirit.

This view impacts Luke's demonology because just as the devil tried to thwart the work of Christ, so he now tries to thwart the work of the church. When Luke wrote about the devil, he viewed him not just as the antagonist of Jesus but also of those who continue Jesus' mission. While this attitude manifests itself strongly in Acts, it also impacted Luke's gospel.

Like Matthew, Luke also worked from Mark's outline but included material of his own. Some familiar themes reappear. Luke mentions demons twenty-three times, and every reference is to an exorcism; furthermore, fourteen of the twenty-three references come from just two chapters (8 and 11—the first dealing with a demoniac and the second with the accusation by some Jews of Jesus' being in league with evil forces). Luke used "devil" and "Satan" interchangeably. He used "Beelzebul" only when he retold Mark's account of those who accused Jesus of being in league with Beelzebul. Nowhere in Acts did he use that term, and no Christian writer after Luke used it either. Clearly the Christian writers were still clarifying and organizing what they had inherited from the Jewish apocryphal writers: one chief enemy who would be referred to either as Satan or the devil (recall that *diábolos* is a Greek translation of the Hebrew word "Satan"). This step represented real progress in understanding or at least in giving shape to the evil forces.

Luke's main portrayal of the devil occurs in his version of the temptation of Jesus (4:1-13). Like Matthew, he added to Mark's account, but Luke revised Matthew's account to provide a brilliant psychological analysis of the devil as tempter.

The devil comes to Jesus in the wilderness and tells him to prove he is the Son of God by commanding a stone to become bread, only to be rebuffed by Jesus. But for Luke this temptation represents the most basic temptation, to physical satisfaction and pleasure.

Next the devil gives Jesus a vision of "all the kingdoms of the world" and offers them to Jesus if he will worship the devil (Luke 4:5).

Note that Jesus does not challenge Satan's claim to have the world in his power. Jesus has here been presented with a higher, more formidable temptation than the mere physical. He can have wealth and power on a grand scale, a dreamed-of goal for many people. But again Jesus refuses.

Now the devil becomes more devious. Jesus has proved his ability to withstand temptation; he has proved himself righteous and holy. The devil turns that achievement into something loathsome: spiritual pride. The devil takes Jesus to the parapet of the Jerusalem temple and urges him to throw himself down. There is no danger there since angels will save him, proving that he is the Son of God. Luke realized that people can elevate their own good acts to a point where they credit themselves rather than God for their goodness (only Luke tells of the technically pious but self-righteous Pharisee who looks down on the publican in 18:9-14). If Jesus hurls himself down, there is no threat to anyone else, he will not be harmed, and he will have proven the devil wrong. But Luke portrays Jesus refusing to fall for even that most seductive temptation. "When the devil had finished every test"—there is nothing worse he can do than suggest spiritual pride—"he departed from him" (Luke 4:13).

Here we see Luke's ecclesiology playing a role. Writing for Christians in the 80s, Luke believed the devil's real threat to the church lay not in displays of power such as possession but in the everyday, subtle temptations to which we all succumb. Luke has theologically "updated" the most primitive Christian notions of the devil.

Luke followed up on the danger of temptation by citing its most sordid success. Mark, Matthew, and Luke all tell of how Judas betrayed Jesus, but only Luke says that "Satan entered into Judas called Iscariot" (22:3). Where the Master triumphed, the disciple failed.

Luke continued his account of the devil's ruthless temptations in the Acts of the Apostles. Luke idealized the earliest community as one in which all people shared their goods equally. But one couple, Ananias and Sapphira, kept back some wealth for themselves. The apostle Peter claimed they were under Satan's power, and they were both struck dead (5:1-11).

Effective as his gospel temptation scene is, Luke mentions "Satan" and "devil" only four times combined in Acts because the work of the Holy Spirit through the apostles is weakening Satan's power. Luke certainly believed in the devil and in the harm he could do, but the evangelist's optimism for the new Christian era caused him to play down Satan's role.

The word "demon" nowhere appears in Acts. As for the devil, Paul encounters him as the force behind the achievements of a magician (13:4-12), while Satan appears as an enemy of the community.

Luke's attitude toward hell mirrored that of Mark and Matthew. He saw it as a place of eternal punishment, although he twice uses the word Hades (10:15; 16:23), the Greek name for the underworld where the deceased suffered for their transgressions. He may have done that to help Gentile converts from paganism to understand his meaning, although Matthew also used that word (11:23).

John

Luke wrote in the 80s of the first century. The fourth and last gospel that would be accepted by Christians into the canon of the New Testament dates around the year 100 and is attributed to one of Jesus' twelve apostles named John. Christian scholars accepted this attribution even into the twentieth century, but no mainline exegete accepts that now.

For one thing, the author of this gospel, "John the apostle," never cites anyone named John as one of the twelve apostles nor does he even provide a list of the Twelve. Readers would never know that, for example, Matthew, Bartholomew, and Philip belonged to the

Twelve. The author does, however, mention a disciple named Nathanael (1:45-49) who appears in no other gospel and who even disappears from this one after the first chapter. If the author of John were one of the Twelve, why does he say almost nothing about them?

The "apostle" John was identified with an obscure figure called the "Beloved Disciple" who rested his head on Jesus' breast at the Last Supper (13:23). But if he were one of the Twelve who traveled about with Jesus for the three years of his ministry (according to this gospel), why does he first appear when Jesus has exactly one day of life left?

This and other evidence convinced scholars that John, whoever he was, wrote about the year AD 100. Not a Galilean fisherman, he was apparently a diasporan Jew who converted to Christianity and lived probably in Roman western Asia Minor (modern Turkey). His gospel contains a great deal of sophisticated theology, especially Christology, and John contributed to Christian demonology.

Yet he does not do so with the event that so engaged Matthew and Luke: the temptation of Jesus in the desert. John simply leaves this story out. He also leaves out Beelzebul; for him and for later writers there would be Satan, the devil, and demons. But even Satan merits only one mention (13:27) when John repeats Luke's account of how Satan entered into Judas; John sets this event at the Last Supper and not before it as Luke does. And as with the other gospels, John treat demons (chs. 7, 8, and 10) in relation to exorcisms and claims by Jesus' enemies that he has a demon. Thus "devil" would be the operative word in this gospel.

But even that word John uses only three times and twice in referring to Judas. When talking to the Twelve, Jesus says that "'one of you is a devil.' He was speaking of Judas" (6:70). This is the only place in the New Testament to call a specific person a devil, and we know that Jesus is using the term figuratively because if John believed Judas were a devil, there would have been no need for Satan to enter into him at the Last Supper. John also separates Satan and this human "devil" at verse 13:2: "The devil had already put it into the heart of Judas son of Simon Iscariot to betray him." Here John follows Luke (22:3). Later generations of Christians would routinely use "devil" in the plural and sometimes apply the term to humans.

John followed the other evangelists in seeing the devil as dominating the world. As part of his Last Supper discourse, Jesus warns his disciples, "the ruler of this world is coming. He has no power over me" (14:30). John does not here use the word "devil," but he was writing after the other gospels and knew their general content, and this fits what happened in their narratives of the devil's temptation of Jesus.

John actually made only one unique reference to the devil, and, sadly, it was a dangerous one.

John's gospel manifests a definite dislike of Jews in general and not, like Matthew, just of the Jerusalem establishment that wanted Jesus' death. In chapter 6 Jesus speaks about the bread of life, and a member of a group identified simply as "the Jews" (6:41-52) challenges some of what he says. Jesus says to the group, "Your ancestors ate the manna in the wilderness . . ." (6:49). *Your* ancestors? Jesus is also a Jew, and the gospels of Matthew and Luke trace his ancestry back to Abraham through the people of the Exodus. He should be saying *our* ancestors. On another occasion (8:17) Jesus says to some scribes and Pharisees, "In *your* law it is written . . . " and he then cites the book of Deuteronomy (8:17). But Deuteronomy, a volume of the Torah believed to have been written by Moses, was sacred to all Jews, including Jesus. The word "your" again separates

Jesus not just from the scribes and Pharisees but from all Jews. As offensive as these examples are, John's anti-Semitism took an even worse turn.

In 8:13-59 Jesus speaks about his Father in heaven. Some Jews challenge him and refer to their father Abraham. Jesus counters with, "You are from *your father, the devil*, and you choose to do from your father's desires. He was a murderer from the beginning and does not stand in the truth, because there is no truth in him. When he lies, he speaks according to his own nature, for he is a liar and the father of lies" (John 8:44).

Part of this is a play on words since at verse 40 Jesus had said that these opponents wanted to kill him, thus linking them to the devil, the murderer "from the beginning." But the key element is the accusation that the father of the Jews is not Abraham but the devil. Scholars cannot be sure what John had in mind when he wrote that odious line, but it would play great role in justifying two millennia of Christian anti-Semitism, especially when joined with that other dangerous verse, Matthew 27:25: "His blood be on us and on our children!"

Possibly the best-known passage in this gospel is its prologue (1:1-18): "In the beginning was the Word." Scholars debate whether this was part of the original gospel or was added after the gospel was written (as was chapter 21). The prologue images Jesus as the "light of all people," and "darkness did not overcome it" (1:5). This theme of light continues throughout the prologue.

The words "in the beginning" obviously recall the opening verses of Genesis when God separates the light from the darkness and sees that the light is good. Since John wrote well after Paul's career, he may have had the New Adam in mind since that would be in keeping with the Genesis theme. But with the development of the idea of hell as a dark pit or an abyss, the word "darkness" may also refer to evil spirits, especially since Jesus returns to the theme of darkness in his last public word to the people. He warns people that if they walk in the darkness, then the darkness could overtake them (12:35-36), but he has come to liberate from darkness those who believe in him (12:45). But John never equates this dark force with the devil.

The Pauline letters and the four gospels have demonstrated several things about the New Testament in general and early Christian belief in the devil in particular. Christians often use the phrase "Scripture speaks with one voice," and, to be sure, it does on some matters. But it also speaks with several voices on others (at least initially). The earliest Christian literature indicates that the first believers did not enunciate a clear demonology. They borrowed heavily from Jewish ideas and, to a lesser extent, Greek ones. Matthew (11:23) and Luke (10:15) even slipped in *Hades*, the Greek word for the underworld as a place of punishment. These first Christians also came up with their own, original understandings, for example, that the world lies in the power of Satan and that Satan attacked Jesus and his movement while he was alive and now, after his death, attacks his church.

Furthermore, we have seen the Christians slowly but surely shedding the many diverse notions and names that came to them from the Jewish apocrypha. Mastema and Semyaza play no role in the New Testament. Belial appears but once (2 Cor 6:15), and while Beelzebul makes seven appearances, all are in the Synoptic Gospels (Mark, Matthew, Luke) and six relate to one incident, an accusation by some Jews that Jesus casts out demons through the power of Beelzebul. By the year 90, after the first three gospels had been written, Beelzebul disappears from the New Testament.

The apostle Paul and the Synoptic evangelists cleared up another matter by virtually restricting the use of the

word "demon" to accounts of exorcism (evangelists) or
pagan gods (Paul), while using "Satan" and "devil" to
refer to the leader of the evil spirits and the main opponent of Jesus and his followers. Finally, in general,
New Testament writers would use "Satan" and "devil"
interchangeably.

But the Christian understanding of the major spiritual enemy of Christ and his church would continue to
develop, and other new evil figures would appear, such
as the Man of Perdition, Antichrist, and 666.

Luke and Lucifer

There was a curious development of Luke's treatment of the devil. In the book of Isaiah, the Old Testament prophet, there is a passage that reads: "How
you are fallen from heaven, O Day Star, son of Dawn!
. . . But you are brought down to Sheol, to the depths
of the Pit" (14:12; 15). The prophet had in mind an
unidentified pagan king and "used an ancient Canaan-
ite myth about a lesser god's attempt to become king
of the pantheon to illustrate the pride of an earthly
king" (Frederick Moriarty, "Isaiah 1–39," *Jerome Biblical Commentary*, 274 OT). At Luke 10:18, Jesus says
that he "watched Satan fall from heaven like a flash of
lightning." Christian scholars, following the lead of the
evangelist Matthew, always searched the Old Testament
for prophetic passages relating to Jesus, and they had
little trouble seeing the link between these two. Isaiah
is the prophet most quoted in the New Testament, especially by two very influential writers, Paul and Matthew,
so this link seemed assured: both prophet and Messiah
had seen an evil being fall from heaven. This may not
have been the best interpretation. Russell points out,
"In the New Testament . . . the bearer of light is the
Christ" (*The Devil*, 299).

By the mid-second century a Palestinian Greek known as Justin the Martyr (d. 165) linked the two passages (H. Kelly, *The Devil at Baptism*, 177). Like all Christian writers of the first century of the church, Justin wrote in Greek.

But in the second century more and more Latin-speaking Christians began producing literature, and naturally the Latin-speaking believers wanted the Bible in their own language. Scholars debate when the first Latin translations were made, but in the late fourth and early fifth century, under the direction of a scholar named Jerome (ca. 350 – ca. 420), the most widely used translation, now known as the Vulgate, came into being.

For the Isaian reference to "bright morning star," the translator used the word "Lucifer," which means "light-bearer" in Latin. Since the verse in Isaiah about "Lucifer" falling from heaven was linked with the verse in Luke about Jesus seeing Satan fall from heaven, "Lucifer" became one more name for Satan. It does not appear in the Bible but has achieved common acceptance as a name for the devil.

CHAPTER SEVEN

The Devil in Later Epistles

The four gospels, Acts, and the authentic epistles of the apostle Paul are the major biblical books for Christians. Proof of that is that a passage from a gospel is read in every Sunday church service, and while churches may draw from a number of New Testament epistles, those of Paul predominate. In sheer volume, these twelve books make up 79 percent of the New Testament; in theological importance, they overwhelm the rest of the New Testament.

Yet there are still fifteen other NT books (three only one page long), and they also contributed to the Christian idea of the devil. All of them postdate Paul's career and the gospel of Mark; most postdate the gospels of Matthew and Luke. This means that the writers of these works—fourteen epistles and the book of Revelation—had been influenced by major works already in circulation. But they are Scripture and deserve a look to see what they taught about the devil.

History also played a great role in the developing Christian understanding of Satan. Jesus died no later than AD 36 when Pontius Pilate was recalled to Rome for incompetence. As a Jew, Jesus would have known

the Old Testament books as well as material from at
least some of the Jewish apocrypha, but decades after
his death and the writing of the New Testament books,
whatever he taught about Satan would have been told,
retold, and developed for new situations.

The two most important new situations were the
continued existence of the community—now becoming
the church—and the movement of Christianity from
Judea into eastern Mediterranean Gentile areas like
Syria and Asia Minor and then into the major Western
areas of Greece and Rome. There is also sketchy evidence of a Christian presence in Egypt and even Roman
Gaul (modern France).

As more and more Christians recognized the church
as the continuation of Christ's work, they likewise
understood the devil as the opponent of the church.
This appears in late New Testament and early noncanonical literature. The Christians particularly believed
that the devil worked through false teachers, while possession faded as a demonic activity.

The Christians experienced hostility in Judea, a hostility that continued as Christian missionaries reached
Jewish diasporan communities. Luke says much about
this in Acts. The situation might have been better in
Gentile areas, but as the Christians moved, they began
to run afoul of Roman authorities. In Acts 19:21-40,
Luke gives a good example of what could happen.

Luke says that Paul enjoyed great success while preaching in Ephesus, a city by the Aegean Sea on the west coast
of Asia Minor, and that he did so by convincing the locals
"that gods made with hands are not gods" (19:26). As
people stopped believing in the gods, they ceased to purchase statues of the city's patron goddess Artemis, statues
made by local silversmiths. The silversmiths objected and
went on to use an argument that won over others—that
is, if the conversions continued they might "reduce the

sanctuary of the great goddess to unimportance" (19:27), that is, hurt the tourism industry.

Although many believers like to think that religion deals with the spiritual and has nothing or little to do with money, in society at large the two are inseparable; consider, for example, all the money necessary for churches' charitable works. The silversmiths and others depended on belief in the goddess for their livelihood, and the new faith threatened that. In the early second century in Asia Minor a Roman governor named Pliny the Younger had to deal with complaints from butchers that as people converted to Christianity, they ceased buying animals to offer as sacrifices in the local temples.

These are but two examples of the problems a new faith could experience, and soon pagans saw threats not just to sales but also to their culture and tradition. Twice in the first century a Roman emperor—Nero in 64 and Domitian in 95—persecuted Christians. Even when not persecuted, the Christians were routinely suspected of crimes, including horrid ones like cannibalism (for both eating flesh and drinking blood) and were often subjected to discrimination. Many Christians understandably saw the hand of the devil in the difficulties they experienced.

As the church became more spread out geographically and increased in membership, church government became necessary. The apostle Paul could write about spiritual leaders such as prophets and people practicing *glossolalia* (speaking in tongues), but the church of the late first century needed more organization. Three offices soon came into being, the *presbúteros* (elder), *diákonos* (deacon), and *epískopos* (bishop).

(These offices evolved over time and should not be equated totally with these offices in modern churches.)

Part of the pastoral care that the men holding these offices performed was to aid Christians in their struggle against Satan. But by the second century the bishops had begun to enunciate Christian teaching on the devil, often by interpreting New Testament passages.

Another crucial historical factor is the absorption by Christians of the Greco-Roman culture into which they had moved. That one sentence covers an enormous amount of ground. Basically it involves a significant reunderstanding of what the faith meant as the increasingly Gentile Christians left Jewish culture behind. For example, all the books of the New Testament were written in Greek, not in a Semitic language. By the third century Christians had so settled into the Gentile culture that they were defining God and Christ with the terms "person," "substance," and "Trinity"—words and ideas found nowhere in the Bible.

In this new Gentile culture the understanding of the devil began to change as well, but the Jewish element continued to be strong.

Let us now turn to the remaining New Testament books.

In the 80s, contemporary with Matthew and Luke, someone claiming to be Paul wrote the Epistle to the Colossians. Colossae was a city in Asia Minor whose Christian community had been founded by Epaphras, a disciple of Paul. This brief epistle never refers to the words demon, devil, or Satan. It does refer (2:15) to "Principalities and Powers," but this occurs in a criticism of Christians who have maintained some Jewish practices. Many ancient Jews believed that angels governed the world, and the reference here is most likely to them and not to Satan, a word not used in Colossians.

At approximately the same time another pseudonymous author claiming to be Paul wrote an epistle with no specific destination but which has become known as the epistle to the Ephesians. It makes two references to the devil (4:27; 6:11), the first warning people, "do not let the sun go down on your anger" (Eph 4:26) because such an attitude would give the devil a foothold. The second reference (6:11) urges believers to "put on the whole armor of God" to resist the wiles of the devil. Both references focus on the devil as tempter.

A third letter from this period claims to be not by Paul but by James, a relative of Jesus and head of the first Jerusalem Christian community. It refers much to the Old Testament and says that the (unknown) community to which it was written met in a synagogue (2:2). Clearly this community had many converts from Judaism. "James" makes one of the few nongospel references to demons (2:19). He worried about Christians who thought that believing in Jesus was sufficient and they had no obligation to do good works. James demolishes that view by pointing out that demons have the same belief that these people do—that is, the demons know that God and his Son exist. This use of "demon" clearly does not refer to pagan gods, and James most likely understood demons as the same evil spirits who possessed people in the gospels.

His lone reference to the devil is a practical, pastoral one : "resist the devil, and he will flee from you" (Jas 4:7).

Paul's letter to the community at Thessalonica is now known as 1 Thessalonians because there is a second letter claiming to be by him, earning it the title 2 Thessalonians. The pseudonymous author of this letter probably wrote in the 80s but to what community is unknown. He had a great interest in the Second Coming and explained what was delaying it: "It cannot happen until the great apostasy has taken place, and the Man of Lawlessness, the Man of Perdition, has appeared" (my translation). This Man will raise himself to a divine level when he comes, but what is he waiting for? "And you too know what is still holding him back from appearing before his appointed time. The mystery of wickedness is already at work, but let him who is restraining it once be removed, and the Man of Perdition will appear openly." But, "The Lord will destroy him with the breath of his mouth" (2 Thess 2:3, 6-8; my translation).

Who is the Man of Perdition? "Paul" refers to an apostasy and links the Man of Perdition to it, so it seems likely that he was a Christian who broke off from "Paul's" community. This pending apostasy may have been so threatening that "Paul" thinks it to be a sign of the end, except that some being is holding the Man of Perdition back. Who is doing this? A good man? An angel? That cannot be determined, but it cannot be God because "Paul" said that the Lord would destroy the Man of Perdition *after* he appeared.

Surely an event like this would be too tempting for Satan to pass up, and, yes, there he is: "The coming of the lawless one is apparent in the working of Satan, who uses all power, signs, lying wonders, and every kind of wicked deception" (2:9). Apostasy threatened the church, and "Paul" believed that one who would raise an apostasy would be in league with Satan. He works against the church as he worked against Jesus and his disciples.

Many later Christians did identify the Man of Perdition—he was the Antichrist. That word does not appear in this epistle but only in the First and Second Epistles of John, and the presentation of Antichrist in those two epistles does not match the Man of Perdition in 2 Thessalonians.

Other authors also wrote in Paul's name. In the 80s someone wrote a combination of moral exhortations and good Christology in a work known as the Epistle to the Hebrews, even though this work does not have the characteristics of an epistle. As for the title, no one can be sure where it originated, although the work was called by that title around the year 200. It makes a single reference to the devil (2:14) in which the author tells his readers that through death Jesus destroyed the devil's power over death, here probably meaning the death of the soul.

Sometime between 100 and 110 came three pseudo-Pauline epistles traditionally grouped together as the Pastoral Epistles (1–2 Timothy, Titus), most likely by the same unknown person but possibly not in the order in which they are placed in the Bible. The supposed recipients are Paul's disciples Timothy (Rom 16:21; 1 Cor 4:17; 2 Cor 1:1) and Titus (2 Cor 2:13; Gal 2:1). The letters add little to our investigation since the three combined use the words "demon," "devil," and "Satan" a grand total of six times with the epistle to Titus not using any of those words and 2 Timothy making just one reference.

As is common in the New Testament books, the writer of these epistles did not speak directly of evil spirits but referred to them in a more general context. By the year 100 the Christians had expanded to areas where the traditional Jewish base for understanding the Scriptures did not exist, and Gentile converts brought new questions and new understandings. More and more the later New Testament books spoke of "false teachers," and in this context we find 1 Timothy's reference to demons.

The author expected the imminent "last times" when "some will renounce the faith by paying attention to deceitful spirits and teachings of demons" (1 Tim 4:1). This is not the traditional use of the word "demon," which usually applied to false pagan deities or spirits that possessed people. Here "Paul" related the demons to false doctrines that will be taken up by those who had been Christians but deserted the faith. He does not relate exactly what doctrines the demons had corrupted but focuses instead on false teaching as a sign of the last times. Many Christian writers would make that link.

For the author of 1 Timothy false teachers also represented just one of the many and multifarious problems of organizing a church, problems that the devil is all too happy to exacerbate. "Paul" recommended discipline to deal with troublemakers: "Among them are men like Hymenaeus and Alexander, whom I have turned over to Satan, so that they may learn not to blaspheme" (1 Tim 1:20). This verse alludes to the authentic Pauline epistle, 1 Corinthians 5:5, where, at that early period, Satan was not totally evil because Paul wanted to "hand this man over to Satan for the destruction of the flesh, so that his spirit may be saved on the Day of the Lord." The author of 1 Timothy makes this allusion primarily to lend authenticity to his pseudonymous epistle, but note that he follows the true Paul by hoping that Alexander and Hymenaus "may learn not to blaspheme" (1:20), that is, they might change their behavior. This also recalls the Old Testament passages where Satan carries out unpleasant work for God. This epistle proves that traditional Jewish ideas about Satan held on for much of the New Testament period.

"Paul" next turns to order in the community. Leaders of the early communities could act in arrogant ways; the author of the Third Epistle of John (*ca.* 110) complained about "Diotrephes who enjoys being in charge" (v.9). To prevent such trouble, the author of 1 Timothy emphasizes the qualities that the presiding officer (*epískopos*) must have, such as being "temperate, sensible, respectable, hospitable" (3:2), but there is more: "He must not be a recent convert, or he may be puffed up with conceit and fall into the condemnation as the devil. Moreover, he must be well thought of by outsiders, so that he may not fall into disgrace and the snare of the devil" (1 Tim 3:6-7).

This is an important verse. For "Paul," the devil has kept pace with the changing situation of the church. In a church that is expanding, entering new geographical areas, and facing problems unknown to the earliest disciples, a good leader is essential. Cleverly, the devil looks for weaknesses in the *epískopos*, taking advantage of a new convert who prides himself upon being in charge of those longtime in the faith and/or of being so focused on governing the community that he ignores its reputation with outsiders.

The devil's attack on good order in the community extends also to widows, who represented an order in the church. In the ancient world, women could help their husbands on the farm or in the shop, but, in general, they could not work outside the home (although in Philippi Paul met a Gentile woman named Lydia who was a dealer in dyes for cloth—Acts 16:14). This meant that many widows found themselves in straightened circumstances if not actually destitute. Christian concern for them went back to the earliest days of the church (Acts 6:1). But such good intention could be taken advantage of, as "Paul" knew: "Honor widows who are really widows" (1 Tim 5:3). He then goes on to enumerate the conditions for true widowhood and the qualities widows should possess. He particularly worries about young widows, who in those days could be as young as seventeen or eighteen. His solution to the problem? "I would have younger widows marry, bear children, and manage their households, so as to give the adversary no occasion to revile us. For some have already turned away to follow Satan" (1 Tim 5:14-15).

Who is the adversary? Not likely to have been a human being since when the New Testament speaks of human enemies, it usually refers to religious opponents of Jesus, Christians who betray their faith, or pagan opponents and persecutors of Christians, and not opponents looking for cheap scandal. The logical identification would be Satan who can use scandal to harm the community. Supporting this is the reference, immediately following, of some young widows who have already turned to Satan. "Paul" does not say how, but in this epistle he expresses great concern about young widows "for when their sensual desires alienate them from Christ, they want to marry [again]" (1 Tim 5:11). The "natural desires" would be for a husband and family but would also include sexual desire.

This passage also strengthens the epistle's claim to authenticity since the historical Paul had written this: "To the unmarried and the widows I say that it is well for them to remain unmarried as I am. But if they are not practicing self-control, they should marry. For it is better to marry than to be aflame with passion" (1 Cor 7:9). Also worth noting is that the true Paul speaks of desires but does not link them to Satan as the pseudo-Paul does in 1 Timothy.

Pseudo-Paul's belief that women should know their place also extended to the archetypal woman. The true Paul and the author of 1 Timothy are the only biblical writers outside of the book of Genesis in the Hebrew Bible to mention Eve by name. But Paul alluded to Eve as part of a warning against false teachers, "[just] as the serpent deceived Eve by its cunning, your thoughts will be led astray from a sincere and pure devotion to Christ. For if someone comes and proclaims another Jesus than the one we proclaimed . . ." (2 Cor 11:3-4). Pseudo-Paul, on the other hand, used Eve to strengthen male control over the community: "I permit no woman to teach or to have authority over a man; she is to keep silent. For Adam was formed first, then Eve; and Adam was not deceived, but the woman was deceived and became a transgressor. Yet she will be saved through childbearing" (1 Tim 2:12-15). Pseudo-Paul did not mention the Eden serpent, much less equate it with Satan, but his section on nubile young widows— that is, women who could be led astray by their desires—parallels his view of Eve.

The last reference to Satan in the Pastoral Epistles occurs in a now familiar context: false teachers. "The Lord's servant must not be quarrelsome but kind to everyone, an apt teacher, patient, correcting opponents with gentleness. God may perhaps grant that they will repent and come to know the truth, and that they may escape from the snare of the devil, having been held captive by him to do his will" (2 Tim 2:25-26).

Before leaving the Pastorals, we must note one odd reference. When "Paul" is talking about the office of *diákonos*, he lists the qualities a deacon's wife should have, such as being sober and reliable, but he also lists what they should not be (1 Tim 3:8-13). English translations usually say that they should not be "gossips" or "slanderers," but the Greek word is *diabólous* or "devils." The translations are correct because Pseudo-Paul is speaking about human beings, not evil spirits. What we have here is a rare scriptural and figurative use of the word, comparable to Jesus' calling Judas a devil in the gospel of John (6:70).

The Pastorals clearly demonstrate how the Christian understanding the devil had changed as the church moved into new areas and new situations. In the gospels, Jesus struggles against evil spirits who possess people and a chief evil spirit who dominates the world. By the turn of the first century, as the church struggled for its place in a new world, the Christians understood the devil very much as a threat to the community, especially via apostates and false teachers.

Paul was not the only person whose name was borrowed by other writers. Somewhere between the years 80 and 90 an unknown author claiming to be Peter, leader of the Twelve, produced the First Epistle of Peter in a location that scholars cannot determine. It makes a single reference to the devil, but this lone reference is a famous one. "Peter" is speaking about personal behavior: "Discipline yourselves, keep alert. Like a roaring lion your adversary the devil prowls around, looking for someone to devour," an image taken from Psalm 22:13 as a symbol of threats to one's goodness. Since by this time the devil had been accepted as a threat to Christians, this adds nothing new to the developing Christian notion of the devil, but it is certainly a vivid image and one with a long Old Testament heritage, such as Psalm 7:2, Deuteronomy 33:22, Jeremiah 2:30, and, of course, Daniel in the lion's den (Dan 6:2-25).

Contemporary with 1 Peter is the Epistle of Jude, which claims as its author a relative of Jesus (Mark 6:3). Like 1 Peter, this epistle makes but a single reference to the devil, but one that has caused much discussion. This short epistle has no chapters, just verses.

"Jude" warns his readers about false teachers who not only preach false doctrine but also ignore the angels, a shocking practice because "when the archangel Michael contended with the devil and disputed about the body of Moses, he did not dare to bring a condemnation of slander against him" (Jude 1:9). When did the devil get into an argument with the archangel Michael about the corpse of Moses? According to the Bible, never. But "Jude" is here citing a Jewish apocryphal work known as the *Assumption of Moses*, and that dates to the first century AD. While this startling verse did not impact Christian belief or teaching about the devil, it does demonstrate the continued influence of Jewish apocryphal literature on the Christian notion of the devil. Supporting this is Jude's open citation of the Jewish apocryphal work, *1 Enoch* (v. 14).

In addition to apocryphal elements there are also traces of even older, biblical notions. Note that archangel Michael was expected to treat Satan with respect and not to use "a condemnation of slander against him." This recalls the Old Testament books that portray Satan carrying out work for God.

About 125 in Asia Minor another writer claiming to be Peter wrote the Second Epistle of Peter, the last New Testament book to be written. By that time the Christians had moved into the Greco-Roman world, and the church was becoming more settled and organized. The Christians continued to respect and use the Old Testament, but they were less comfortable with nonbiblical Jewish literature. "Peter" never used "demon," "devil," or "Satan," but he did rewrite (2:10-22) Jude's denunciation of the false teachers, and he left out the now awkward references to Jewish apocryphal literature. For him Christian beliefs and teachings on the devil rely on the Old Testament and not on other Jewish literature, at least openly. In fact, Jewish apocryphal notions of Satan continued to play a quiet but significant role in Christian theology.

Antichrist

Three small epistles—two barely a page long—known as 1, 2, and 3 John were composed around 110 in western Asia Minor. The name John does not appear in any of them, but ancient and medieval scholars thought one person wrote all of them, and they found similarities between the Gospel of John and 1 John, the longest of the three letters. Since the gospel had been written by John the apostle, the first letter must have been written by him, and since the same person wrote all three, and so on. In 2 and 3 John the author self-identifies as "the Presbyter," that is, the elder, and since *presbúteroi* were men, we know that a man wrote these epistles. Since the same person most likely wrote all three epistles, we can speak of an elder but definitely not of an apostle as the author.

We may discount the third epistle which does not mention "devil," "demon," or "Satan," and refers only twice to evil (vv. 10, 11) and uses it in the sense of immoral behavior. Second John likewise makes no mention of these three titles, but it does join 1 John in having had great influence on the Christian concept of evil and of evil beings. Here are the relevant citations:

- 1 John 2:18-19: Children, it is the last hour. As you have heard that *Antichrist* is coming, so now many *Antichrists* have come. From this we know that this is the last hour. They went out from us, but they did not belong to us.

- 1 John 2:22: This is the *Antichrist,* the one who denies the Father and the Son.

- 1 John 4:2-3: Every spirit that confesses that Jesus Christ has come in the flesh is from God, and every spirit that does not confess Jesus is not from God. And this is the spirit of the *Antichrist.*

- 2 John 1:7: Many deceivers have gone out into the world, those who do not confess that Jesus Christ has come in the flesh; any such person is the deceiver and the *Antichrist!*

The word "Antichrist" can mean "against Christ" or "in place of Christ." How is the term used here? John first refers to the Antichrist in the singular, and he appears to be a more than human figure since his coming is linked to "the final hour," unless he is an extensively powerful human being who means to harm the Christians, such as Nero or Domitian come back to life since a deceased emperor who returned to life would be a more than human figure.

But the second reference speaks of Antichrists in the plural and refers to former members of the community, who, now that they have broken into schism, are recognized for never having been true members.

The third reference returns to the singular, but now Antichrist is one who denies that Jesus is the Christ and also denies both the Father and the Son—two essential Christian beliefs. Clearly the author is here worried about false teaching because he goes on to urge his readers, "Let what you heard from the beginning abide in you" (1 John 2:24). Evidently this was a community in deep trouble, dealing with false teaching and schism, both caused by humans.

The fourth reference moves beyond the human to a spirit, but this spirit is also characterized by false teaching since it "does not acknowledge Jesus Christ come in human nature." The third reference referred to denying Jesus is the Christ while this reference speaks of denying his human nature, but both deal with false teaching. The second "false teaching" reference may echo the prologue to John's gospel, which speaks of the Word being made flesh (1:1)—an essential element of human nature.

The fifth reference, from 2 John, also refers to those who deny that Jesus came in human nature. But whereas the second citation, referring to the schismatics, uses the plural form Antichrists, here the author bundles them together into one: "they are the deceiver, they are the Antichrist." Here John is using the word as in "they are the enemy" because he has already referred to many deceivers.

It is difficult to reconcile all these references. The initial reference suggests a more than human figure whose arrival will signal the end, but then John switches from the uncertain end to practical problems, false teaching and schism, with the former probably causing the latter.

This would also explain why he can use the plural "Antichrists," since they are all "against Christ."

While none of these citations refer to Satan, the citation that contrasts the "spirit" who *acknowledges* Jesus with the "spirit" who *denies* him may suggest good and evil spirits. But we must be careful because the earliest Christians believed in many spiritual manifestations within people that caused them to accept the faith and to speak within the community. In closing his advice about marriage to the Corinthians, Paul famously said, "I think I too have the Spirit of God" (1 Cor 7:40), meaning his teaching is reliable. These two conflicting spirits John speaks of could have been members of the two struggling parties in his community.

But this vague, unexplained term, Antichrist, certainly has mystery and vitality, and we can see why later generations of Christians would seize upon it and apply it to their enemies, especially other Christians. Nowhere is Antichrist linked with Satan, the Man of Perdition, or the elusive 666. 1 John does not contain the words "demon" or "Satan," and its four uses of the word "devil" appear in 3:8-10, a chapter in which the word "Antichrist" does not appear.

CHAPTER EIGHT

The Book of Revelation

For most Christians, Revelation is *the* book about the devil, but, as usual, the matter is more complicated.

First, the title. The Greek name for this book is *Apokálypsis* or Apocalypse—actually, it is the "Apocalypse of John," which means "revelation given to John." But this is a special kind of revelation, a vision given to a seer about some great work God is about to undertake. In the New Testament, this makes the book of Revelation very special, but not so in the ancient world.

Earlier on we looked at some Jewish apocryphal literature, and some of that literature is apocalyptic (for example, the *Apocalypse of Abraham* and the *Apocalypse of Adam*). Scholars have also identified apocalyptic material in the biblical books of Isaiah and Daniel. Apocalyptic was a Jewish literary genre widely known in the ancient world. How well known? A carpenter's son from the tiny town of Nazareth in the backward Jewish province of Galilee knew it well enough to predict to his chosen disciples how the time of tribulation would come, complete with stars falling from the sky (Jesus' entire apocalyptic message takes up all of Mark, chapter

13; there are parallel passages in Matthew 24:15-44 and Luke 21:7-28).

Paul also had apocalyptic expectations. In 1 Thessalonians 4:13-18 he describes what would later be called the Rapture. The pseudonymous author of 1 John thought the appearance of Antichrist would usher in "the final hour" (2:18), while the pseudonymous author of 2 Thessalonians believed the Man of Perdition would usher it in (2:1-12). Apocalyptic thinking and ideas can be found in many places in the New Testament outside the book of Revelation.

But there is more. Just as the Jews produced apocryphal works, so too did Christians. As noted earlier, the most influential has been the second-century Syrian *Protogospel of James*, which provided the names of the parents of Jesus' mother Mary. But many other apocryphal gospels survive—such as the provocative *Gospel of Mary Magdalene* and the notorious *Gospel of Judas*—along with apocryphal epistles, books of acts, and, most important, apocalypses, including ones attributed to Peter, Thomas, and Paul. The biblical book of Revelation is just one of several early Christian apocalypses. It is not a blueprint for the end of the world as so many Christians have believed over the centuries but a canonical example of a widespread, ancient literary genre. Its claim to uniqueness resides solely in its being the only example of a full-fledged apocalypse in the New Testament, *Deo gratias*.

That this visionary book does not contain a blueprint for the end can be shown in a number of ways, but two will make the case.

First, despite the endless predictions by people over the millennia—and even today—who thought that their era was so sinful and hopeless that the end as described in Revelation was surely approaching, the world has stubbornly refused to end.

Second, if Revelation contains a physical description of the end, then the particulars in the book should make sense, but they do not.

- Revelation 6:13—"the stars of the sky fell to the earth"
- Revelation 12:4—"his tail swept down a third of the stars of heaven"

But if the stars had fallen from the sky in chapter 6, how did they get back into the sky to fall for a second time in chapter 12?

The author of Revelation said "I was in ecstasy" (1:10; my translation), and we must take him at his word. This is a visionary book, not a cosmic weather forecast, and we will better comprehend the book when we examine its contents as visionary. We must also understand that although the Apocalypse says much about Satan, the author was not writing a treatise on him but rather fitting Satan into his understanding of the end.

The author of Revelation identifies himself as John (1:2) but does not identify his status in the church—apostle? elder? prophet? Clearly he had some status since he expects the seven churches to which he is writing to pay attention to his words. Scholars often refer to him as John the Seer to distinguish him from the author of the Gospel of John and the author of the three epistles of John.

Scholars date this work around 95, partly because John was on Patmos, a Roman prison island, for what he called "hardships" that the Christians to whom he was writing had shared, which suggests a persecution. The emperor Domitian (81–96) had persecuted some Christians in the city of Rome around 95. Ephesus, home of one of the churches to which John was writ-

ing, also housed a gigantic statue of Domitian, proof of
his importance to the locals who may have followed the
emperor in persecuting Christians.

The seven churches that received these revelations
were all in western Asia Minor, an area evangelized by
Paul. This was Gentile territory but also home to diasporan Jews who would have understood an apocalyptic
text.

John the Seer wrote to the "angels" of the churches,
reminiscent of the Jewish idea of angels as guardians of
communities and, here, symbols of the churches. He
starts off by claiming that the Lord spoke to him and
said, "I am the Alpha and the Omega [the Beginning and
the End]" (1:8), a symbol of the book's constant references to Genesis as well as to the end, again something
that Jewish converts would understand. The church at
Smyrna had difficulty with the local Jews, whom John
denounced as belonging to "a synagogue of Satan" (2:9),
reminiscent of the Gospel of John's negative portrayal of
Jews who do not accept Christianity. But the situation is
actually worse: "the devil is about to throw some of you
into prison" (2:10), thus linking the devil with the persecutors, a theme that had a long future.

The situation was worse in Pergamum "where Satan's throne is" (2:13). Is this meant to be symbolic of
the local church's (perceived) corruption or does it refer
to a pagan deity venerated there? In this place "where
Satan lives," Christians had already been executed for
their faith.

John blasted the church at Thyatira for tolerating
a prophetess whom he labels "Jezebel," a pagan queen
of Israel and the evil woman *par excellence* among the
Jews. Those who have accepted her teachings learned
"the deep things of Satan" (2:24), which John does not
explain, but he links with Satan those who disagree with
him, a practice of the Qumran Jews and, unfortunately,

future Christians. He may also have been thinking of
Eve who believed she would learn the secret of being divine from the serpent, then widely thought to be Satan.

John used the phrase "synagogue of Satan" a second
time, in his letter to the church at Philadelphia (3:9),
again indicating difficulties between the local Christians
and Jews.

The three opening chapters of Revelation are com-
prised of John's introduction of himself and the letters
to the seven churches, but these chapters also make
clear the writer's genuine concern about Satan and his
willingness to attribute to Satan many of the problems
afflicting those churches.

Now John turns to the heart of the book: his visions
of the end (chs. 6–11). These visions include some very
famous passages such as Christ as the Lamb and the
seven seals and the seven trumpets. But none of these
chapters mention the words "devil" or "Satan." The
number seven naturally recalls the opening chapters
of Genesis, here contrasting creation and destruction,
but we must note that as the end commences, *all the
destruction is caused by God*. This is in keeping with
the Old Testament deity who slays the innocent along
with the guilty as, for example, in the Noachic flood and
the killing of the Egyptian children in the tenth plague.
Those Christians who worry about what the devil might
do at the end should be a lot more worried about God!

In all these chapters the Seer made but a single reference to demons, equating them with "idols of gold and
silver and bronze and stone and wood, which cannot
see or hear or walk" (9:20). As we saw earlier, this traditional view went back to the prophet Isaiah and was
held by Paul.

The devil returns in chapter 12 with the famous
vision of the woman "clothed with the sun, with the
moon under her feet, and on her head a crown of twelve

stars" (12:1). The woman most likely represents the church, pregnant with the future of mankind symbolized by the child she is about to bear. The symbolism here is difficult because the church exists when John is writing and he is writing about the future. Some scholars, mostly Catholic, once thought the woman was Jesus' mother Mary, but this book deals with the end and Jesus had already been born, so how could he be the child? Scholars debate this point endlessly, but most likely the child symbolizes the Christians born to mother church.

(Verse 12:17 says that after its defeat, the dragon "was angry with the woman, and went off to make war on the *rest of her children*." Since Catholics believe that Mary bore only one child, the identification of the woman with Mary is difficult to sustain.)

Suddenly there appears "a great red dragon" who wishes to devour the child as soon as it is born (12:2-4) and whom John identifies as "the Devil and Satan" (12:9). The dragon threatens the woman's child, but God rescues them. "And now war broke out in heaven; Michael and his angels fought against the dragon," who fought back with his angels but suffered defeat (12:7).

The identity of the woman is one of many difficulties this passage has presented to Christians for millennia. John wrote about the end of the world, but most modern Christians believe this battle between Satan and Michael occurred before the creation of the world, a view enshrined in much Christian art and even in great literature, such as John Milton's *Paradise Lost*. Ironically, John borrowed this combat idea from Jewish apocryphal books that set the combat at the beginning of the world and resulted in the defeated angels being expelled from heaven and exiled to earth, exactly what happens here: "The great dragon . . . was thrown down to the earth, and his angels were thrown down with him"

(12:9). Why John went against his Jewish sources and moved this to the end of the world is unclear, but generations of Christians have tried to keep both interpretations by taking Revelation as a guide to the end while still placing this cosmic battle before time. As Jeffrey Russell pointed out, "The inconsistency of these stories [about Michael and Satan] is inherited from Apocalyptic Judaism, and *it is irresoluble*" (*The Devil*, 242–43; emphasis added). Christians would do well to heed this scholar's wise words.

In this passage John the Seer makes an important assertion that would change Christianity forever: "The great dragon, the primeval serpent, known as the devil or Satan, who had led all the world astray" (12:9; my translation). The word "primeval" means at the beginning of time, and the only serpent mentioned at the beginning of time was the one who tempted Eve. Also, since Adam and Eve represented "the whole world," by leading them astray the serpent effectively led "the whole world astray." Jewish literature had hinted that the Eden serpent could be Satan, and some Christian writings may imply it, but here John makes it clear.

To be sure, just because John said this does not mean that it necessarily represents Christian teaching—it is, after all, only one verse—but in fact it proved decisive. Future Christians would accept the identification of the Eden serpent with Satan, taking a visionary book as a reliable source for biblical interpretation.

John continues: "And I saw a beast rising out of the sea . . . the dragon gave it his power and his throne and great authority" (13:1-2). In effect, the dragon, Satan, withdraws from the scene while the beast takes over and performs multitudinous evil acts, including persecuting the faithful (13:7). Since "the whole earth followed the beast" (13:3), most scholars believe this refers to the Roman Empire.

But just as the dragon had a deputy, so did the beast. "Then I saw another beast that rose out of the earth" (13:11), followed by an account of the second beast's evil deeds. John does not identify the beast directly but gives his readers what he apparently thought was a helpful clue: "This calls for wisdom: let anyone with understanding calculate the number of the beast, for it is the number of a person. Its number is six hundred sixty-six" (13:18).

666

This number has caused confusion for Christians for two millennia. Many people think it refers to the devil, but this is impossible because the verse says "it is the number of a human being." Satan is not a human being but a spiritual one, so it cannot refer to him.

Others think it applies to the Antichrist, but, as we saw, that word appears only in the epistles 1 and 2 John. In past centuries, when people thought that the apostle John wrote the Gospel of John, the three Johannine epistles, and Revelation, this might have made some sense because the same author would have been involved in all the literature. But modern scholars deny the same authorship to all of these books. Furthermore, even if one accepts the same authorship of all the literature, there are still problems identifying the Antichrist as the person symbolized by 666. For example, in 2 John the author warns about the Antichrist but identifies him with "one bringing different doctrine" (v. 10) and tells people not to admit him to their community. The epistle writer was not speaking of the end but of a very practical problem: false teaching. Nowhere in the epistle is there a reference to an apocalyptic scenario.

So if 666 is not Satan or the Antichrist, then who is he?

The number 666 is composed of Arabic numerals, but in Revelation John the Seer wrote the number out in Greek letters. Why? Because the ancient Jews, Romans, and Christians did not know of Arabic numerals and so they used letters to stand for numerical values. In our own society there are remnants of this practice in the use of Roman numerals, such as Super Bowl XLVIII to stand for Super Bowl 48 or in putting III at the end of a name to signify that the current holder of that name is third in the family to do so.

This approach looks cumbersome, but it obviously worked because ancient peoples used it for centuries. But using letters to represent numerical values produced an odd side effect. While people would choose a name such as Sarah or Isaac because they wanted that name for their child, it was possible to add up the letters in a name to get a numerical value and to give the child a name of some significance. The Jews practiced *gematria*, trying to find a numerical value that might have some symbolic importance. The Hebrew word for "life" has two letters whose numerical value is eighteen, which caused many ancient Jews to consider eighteen a lucky number. Since apocalyptic was a Jewish literary genre, and since John the visionary knew Jewish apocryphal literature, scholars believe that 666 is the sum of the letters in someone's name and thus it might be possible to work from the sum back to the name.

That sounds daunting on the surface but is even worse when one tries it. To stick to Roman numerals, suppose someone's name included this combination of letters: *xiv*. We know that this combination stands for the Arabic number 14. Or does it? To be sure, when we use *xiv*, we mean fourteen, because we assign a value of ten to *x* and a value of four to *iv*. But suppose we add up the letters individually. The letter *x* represents ten, the letter *i* represents one, and the letter *v* represents five.

But $10 + 1 + 5 = 16$, not 14. This small example demonstrates the difficulty of trying to determine names by using the letters that represent numerical values.

We still want to know whom John the Seer understood 666 to be, and scholars have tried to determine that in a number of ways, some quite ingenious. But this book is about Satan, not numerology, so let us go to the most widespread scholarly conclusion.

In Hebrew, the words "Nero Caesar" have a numerical value of 666. That sounds simple, but there are several objections. For example, John wrote in Greek, so how were his readers to know that he wanted them to interpret the number in Hebrew? Also, as emperor, Nero's name was actually Nero Claudius Caesar Augustus Germanicus. But Nero Caesar does work, and it makes much sense. In the eastern Mediterranean, where the book of Revelation was written, there was a widespread belief that Nero, who died in AD 68, either was not really dead or would come back from the dead to wreak vengeance upon his enemies, who would include the Christians. Converts from Judaism would have understood that.

The key here is that 666 must be interpreted in a first-century context—that is, what did the people to whom John wrote think he meant by this number? That has not, of course, prevented people from applying the number willy-nilly to any number of people, including President Ronald Wilson Reagan (count up the letters in each of his names; Fuller, 166).

The End

After 666 the words "devil" and "Satan" are not used again by John the Seer until chapter 20 when the final battle begins. "Then I saw an angel coming down from heaven, holding in his hand the key to the bottomless

pit and a great chain. He seized the dragon, that ancient
serpent, who is the Devil and Satan, and bound him for
a thousand years. . . . When the thousand years are
ended, Satan will be released from his prison and will
come out to deceive the nations at the four quarters
of the earth" (20:1-2, 7-8). Then he will be "thrown
into the lake of fire and sulfur . . . and [he] will be tor-
mented day and night forever and ever" (20:10). Importantly, here the Seer has identified the devil as the Eden
serpent for a second time, confirming that identification, at least for him and his readers.

The Latin word for "thousand years" is *millennium*,
a religious term often used for the end of the world,
such as Y2K in the year 2000. This passage fosters the
belief that the devil will be released from hell to cause
worldwide destruction. This is not a misinterpretation;
John probably meant just that, but, of course, it did not
happen. But John made it clear that the devil will be
sent to the Abyss—recalling the Old Testament Sheol,
the "Pit"—and then, a thousand years later, to an eternal punishment, although John did not here use the
word "hell." In fact, he never used the word at all in this
book.

When the devil and his followers have been defeated,
"the one who sat on [a great white throne]" causes the
earth and sky to vanish (20:11), and God judges all the
dead, "great and small" (20:12)—that is, the Last Judgment—after which there will be (to use another Genesis-
based image) "a new heaven and a new earth" (21:1).
Next comes a description of the New Jerusalem with its
pearly gates and streets of gold.

The Seer finished his work with a warning to scribes
copying the book: "if anyone adds to them [the book's
prophecies], God will add to that person the plagues
mentioned in this book; if anyone takes away from the
words of the book of this prophecy, God will take away

that person's share in tree of life [Gen 1:9] and in the holy city, which are described in this book" (22:18-19).

What does the book of Revelation tell us about the earliest Christian belief in the devil? Before considering that, we must recall that this is a visionary, not a theological, account. Additionally, the author is writing about the end, and he spends much time linking the end with the creation, deliberately using Genesis themes and motifs and the fitting the devil into them rather than providing a coherent demonology.

Some of the themes are traditional ones that we have seen in other New Testament books.

John the Seer does not use the word "Beelzebul," instead using just "Satan" and "devil," continuing a trend found in the gospels.

The devil is a fallen angel and a leader of other fallen angels. He works against the Christian communities in western Asia Minor, sometimes so successfully that John can speak of a synagogue of Satan. He also works with the enemies of Christianity—the Jews, the Romans, and Christians with whom the Seer disagrees, in effect demonizing the Seer's perceived enemies. The pagans worship demons in the form of idols (9:20). The devil will endure eternal punishment.

But John the Seer also advanced the Christian concept of Satan on several levels.

First, he explained a puzzling problem. Jesus had come to redeem the world from evil, but he had died, risen, and returned to heaven, and evil still continued. John spoke of a future judgment of all the people who had ever lived. After this judgment would come the end of the world as we know it, the punishment of Satan, and new heaven and earth. John effectually created the notion of a Last Judgment as a general judgment for all humanity. We do not know if this was original to him or common by the time he wrote, but he did explain the delay in the end of evil with this future reckoning.

His reference to the idols as demons follows a tradition dating back to Paul, but John wrote as the church was entering the Gentile world and converting more and more pagans. Rejecting the notion that the pagan gods are simply nonexistent, John spurs on the belief that while they do exist, they are not deities but demons.

The Seer also provided important physical imagery for Satan as the great red dragon (12:3). Since a dragon is basically a gigantic serpent, John clearly borrowed the image from the Eden account, but nonetheless he did provide a potent and long-lasting visual.

His clear identification of Satan with the Eden serpent was borrowed from Jewish apocryphal books, but John gave it a boost in Christian circles. For twenty centuries (and counting) Christians would accept that identification.

Finally, he treated good and evil as absolutes. We experience evil in a mixed way, seeing both good and evil mixed in persons and institutions. John the Seer demonstrated that between absolute good and absolute evil there is nothing in common.

All in all, this troubled visionary greatly impacted the early Christian understanding of Satan.

CHAPTER NINE

The Early
Christian Creation of Satan

The earliest Christians, such as Paul and John the Seer, believed that the end was nigh upon them. Planning for the future was superfluous at best. But, very inconveniently, the world did not end, and as the decades passed Christians realized that they had to prepare themselves to live in the world for an indefinite time. This realization appears in a number of ways, most obviously with the replacement of charismatic ministries with more quotidian but effective ones such as presbyter, deacon, and bishop.

But another movement was occurring. When Christians in the New Testament referred to the Bible, they meant what their descendants call the Old Testament. But as they settled into the world, they began to speculate whether some of the books they had produced also deserved to be designated as Scripture. The New Testament itself offers hints of this. The Second Epistle of Peter refers to "our brother Paul" and "all his letters" (3:15-16), so the pseudonymous author was aware of a collection of the apostle's letters. Regrettably we do not know to which letters "Peter" was referring, who had prepared the collection or where, and when this preparation had taken place. But 2 Peter proves there was a collection of Paul's letters by about 125.

More than that, "Peter" refers to these letters as *graphé*, using the Greek word for Scripture, for example, as used by Jesus in Mark 12:10. This means that in some circles Christians were valuing their own books as inspired, and this trend became widespread by 150.

From the second to the fourth century various Christian writers would produce various "canon lists," that is, a list of books they believed belonged to what would be called the "New Testament," a phrase initially used around 200 by a writer known as Clement of Alexandria. In 367 Athanasius, patriarch of Alexandria, first produced the list of twenty-seven books that now form the New Testament.

The new canon reshaped Christianity, especially Christian devotion and theology, and literally thousands of books have been written to describe it, explain it, and draw meaning from it.

But the canon also presents a slight drawback because every so often one sees or hears the phrases, "the New Testament view of . . ." or "the New Testament teaching on. . . ." While there are many issues where those phrases could apply, collecting all the inspired, Christian-authored books into a canon can give a false impression of exact unity in teaching; one may ask, if all these books are inspired, how can they not teach the exactly same thing?

While there is indeed a general unity among the books, modern scholarship has demonstrated a considerable variety in belief and teaching among the New Testament works, ranging from minor ones to even the most important. To be sure, they do not offer contradictory teachings, but they do differ.

We should thus be careful in speaking of the "New Testament teaching" on the devil. Many writers mentioned Satan, and they often agreed, but as we briefly review what the New Testament books taught, we will see some diversity and some development.

1. For the earliest Christians Satan existed. Many modern Christians who feel uncomfortable with belief in the devil would like to understand him as a symbol of evil rather than an actual person. They can certainly do that, but they cannot say that the Christians of the New Testament era saw him that way. He existed. Period.

2. Borrowing heavily from Jewish apocryphal literature, the early Christians understood him to be an angel who had fallen from heaven.

3. They presented him as the leader of a host of other fallen angels, again borrowing from the Jews, although the Christians insisted on just one name for this leader, unlike the Jews who cited Semyaza, Mastema, and Azazel.

4. Christian writers did cite names other than Satan but only occasionally. Paul made a single reference to Belial (2 Cor 6:15), and no other Christian writers referred to him at all. Mark's gospel referred to Beelzebul once (3:22), when Jerusalem scribes questioned the source of Jesus' power. Matthew used this name three times but two times were in his version of Mark's account (12:24-27), and the third time as part of Jesus' instruction to his disciples (10:25). Luke likewise used the term three times but only in his version of Mark's account (11:15-19). No other New Testament writer used either of these two names, which simply died out over the decades.

5. Although later Christian writers would use the terms demon and devil interchangeably, in the

New Testament the word "demon" most frequently refers to demonic possession or to pagan deities. Paul used the word "demon" exactly four times to refer to pagan deities, and all four examples appear in two verses of a single epistle (1 Cor 10:20-21).

6. The preferred terms were "Satan" and "devil"— that is, the Hebrew word *Satan* used as a proper noun and the Greek translation of that word as *diábolos*.

7. Many New Testament writers generally, and the evangelists particularly, emphasized Satan's ability to possess people, that is, to take over their bodies physically and to force them to do the will of the evil spirit. Possession could only be cured by an exorcism. There were Jewish exorcists at that time, but the gospels present Jesus as the foremost exorcist.

8. Although horrifying, possession was rare (except early in Mark's gospel, cf. 1:32), and the devil's real threat to Christians was temptation to sin. To stress the importance of this and to demonstrate that Satan's wish to get people to sin knew no bounds, Mark, Matthew, and Luke all include accounts of Satan's temptation of Jesus himself.

9. Paul in his epistles, several other anonymous or pseudonymous authors, and Luke in the Acts of the Apostles all make it clear that, after Jesus' death, Satan did not depart from this world but transferred his evil work, especially temptation, to Jesus' followers.

10. Several New Testament writers following the Jews of Qumran saw fellow believers with whom they disagreed as being in league with Satan, for example, the Man of Perdition in 2 Thessalonians 2:3-12.

11. Perceived enemies of the Christians were also believed to be in league with Satan, such as the Romans (not named directly) in the book of Revelation and, sadly, the Jews in the Gospel of John (ch. 8).

12. Satan and his angels will end up in hell at the end of time (Rev 20:7-10), a place that had been prepared for them (Matt 24:41), so no New Testament writer had to explain how the devil and his followers could both be in hell and roaming about the world. Later writers and many modern Christians believe that God sent the evil angels to hell before he even created the world, a belief with little biblical foundation to support it.

13. Many New Testament writers spoke of a Day of Judgment, and the gospels quote Jesus' discourse on that topic (Mark 13:5-3; Matt 24:4-36; Luke 21:8-36), but the fullest description of the Last Judgment, as this event came to be called, was by John the Seer in the book of Revelation (20:11-15 as part of a larger account of the end).

14. No New Testament writer gave a visual depiction of the devil. Many people in the New Testament, especially Jesus, interact with Satan, but no description survives of him or demons or, for that matter, of angels. Writers used vivid imagery about him, most famously in the First Epistle of Peter as "a roaring lion" (5:8) and in Revelation (12:3) as a great red dragon. Paul said (2 Cor 11:14) that Satan could disguise himself as an angel of light, a phrase that basically said he could take on any appearance that he liked, thus encouraging Christian artists of later ages to portray Satan in any appearance that *they* liked.

15. The devil is not the only evil figure in the New Testament. For example, there is the Man of Perdition (2 Thessalonians), the Antichrist (1–2 John), and 666 (Revelation). The Bible associates the Man of Perdition and 666 with Satan but does not identify either as Satan. Although later writers would do so, 1 and 2 John do not associate the Antichrist with Satan.

16. John the Seer twice identified Satan as the "primeval serpent who had led all the world astray"—that is, the serpent in the Garden of Eden was the devil (Rev 12:9, 20:2; my translation). This identification would significantly determine how Christians understood the Garden of Eden and the Fall.

17. Last and most important, Christianity, like Judaism, is a monotheistic religion (not dualistic), and despite all of Satan's power, he is always under God's power. To be sure, this presents Christians with the significant problem of why God does not curb or eliminate Satan's power, but, and this is important for believers in any era, the New Testament asserts and confirms the monotheistic character of Christianity and of God's dominance. Satan will never completely triumph.

This rather long list makes it seem as if the New Testament writers had covered just about everything, but the early Christian understanding of Satan had a long way to go. When the New Testament books were gaining authority and especially after the establishment of the canon when those books were unequivocally accepted as inspired Scripture, Christian writers could not go against New Testament teaching. But they had little trouble going beyond it and, occasionally, few scruples in doing so.

Much of the Christian development of thinking about the devil, which from here on we will call demonology (the most commonly used term today), resulted from an immense cultural shift in the second and third centuries.

Jesus, his earliest disciples (including Paul), and all the New Testament writers (except Luke) were Jews, as were most believers. But thanks to Paul and other, now anonymous missionaries, Christianity spread into areas that were culturally Greek and Roman. These Gentile Christians, who became a majority no later than 150, took a very different approach to the faith than their Jewish predecessors.

Consider some prominent examples. Anyone reading Paul's letters, especially Galatians and Romans, can see his obsession with the Jewish Law and its relation to Christianity. But by the year 200 only a handful of Jewish Christians worried about that. Most Christians saw the Law as irrelevant or even negative, and the latter attitude would grow over the centuries.

The word *Christós* meant "Messiah" to the first Jewish disciples, who then had to rethink their understanding of the Messiah from a conquering hero to a suffering servant. Gentile Christians had no interest in a Jewish Messiah. If anything, they considered the term a negative because the Jewish leader Bar Kokhba, who led a revolt against Rome (132–35), was revered by his followers as the Messiah.

To cite a theological example of this Jewish to Gentile cultural change, in the gospels the phrase "Son of Man" had apocalyptic overtones, but by the fifth century, when few if any Christians cared about apocalyptic attitudes, great scholars such as Cyril of Alexandria (d. 444) thought that phrase "Son of Man" referred to Jesus' human nature.

Such a vast cultural shift and such new attitudes toward biblical themes and elements inevitably impacted Christian understanding of the devil.

But when we leave the Bible, we also leave the revelatory source accepted by all Christians, and the focus of this book is on what we all accept. Therefore, we will look at later writers only in terms of how they impacted or even changed the biblical understanding of Satan, a process that often obscured the biblical Satan for modern believers. (Readers wishing to follow the story in detail should consult titles listed in the bibliography, especially those by Russell and Henry Kelly.)

Clement of Rome headed the Christian community in the imperial capital, and around 95 he wrote a letter to the community in Corinth, Greece, his only surviving writing. In this letter he blames "the Adversary" for tempting people to commit sins. He uses a familiar image of Satan but does not develop it.

A Syrian bishop, Ignatius of Antioch, was sent to Rome around 115 to be thrown to the lions in the arena. On his trip he wrote several letters to Christian communities. He considers Satan to be the ruler of this age—that is, until the end—and Satan and his evil angels try to thwart the work of Christ. But Ignatius found a particularly evil action on the devil's part. To a community in Smyrna he wrote, "A man who acts without the knowledge of the bishop is serving the devil" (*To the Smyrnaeans*, 9)—that is, disagreement with episcopal authority reflects demonic influence and threatens order in the community, which is an echo of the old chaos/cosmos theme. The devil also encourages heretics who disagree with the bishops and people who leave the community rather than submit to the bishop's authority.

Ignatius floated another idea that would have a long history: God hid the birth of Jesus from Satan via the virginal conception by Mary so that Satan did not realize until it was too late that the one who would redeem the world from evil had come to earth and was an adult. That speculation has no Scriptural justification, an early proof that Christians would not be loath to go well beyond biblical teaching on Satan.

Bishop Polycarp of Smyrna was martyred by the Romans circa 156. In a letter to the church at Philippi (ch. 7), he wrote, "Anyone who does not believe that Christ came in the flesh is an antichrist, and whoever does not witness to the Cross of Christ is of the devil," because the cross would be meaningless if Jesus did not have a body. The first part of the sentence echoes 1 John 4:2-3, that is, the term "Antichrist" can apply to more than one person. But the second part is original to Polycarp—that is, the link between Satan and Antichrist—which is not in Scripture but repeated by many later Christian authors.

Contemporary with Polycarp was a Palestinian Gentile named Justin, known as Justin the Martyr because he died for the faith at Rome circa 165. He witnesses to the difficulty of trying to reconcile Christian belief with the devil and Jewish apocryphal literature. Justin ventured that there were demons in the world, but at the beginning of time these demons had mated with human women, making their current progeny half human and half demon. This made little sense and would signal to later Christian writers that the using Jewish apocryphal writings could present problems.

Justin also reaffirmed the teaching of the book of Revelation that the Eden serpent was actually Satan.

Justin grew up a pagan and spent his life trying to win over pagans to Christianity, partly by dispelling pagan charges against the Christians, such as cannibalism (eating a body, drinking blood) and by explaining what Christians actually believed. He saw paganism at its worst, and he strongly taught that the pagan gods were genuine demons who were in league with Satan to thwart the good work of the Christians. Fitting for

one who died a martyr, Justin argued that although the
demons deluded people with magic and charms, their
chief attack on Christianity was urging the Romans to
persecute.

Justin had philosophical training, the first of many
Christian writers to have such a background. As more
educated people became Christian, they asked many
questions about the faith, including ones about Satan.
A Syrian named Tatian, circa 180, accepted the notion
of sinful angels expelled from heaven. He went on to
say that because they lost contact with God, they ceased
having purely spiritual bodies and thus had grosser,
physical ones. (Were the "spiritual" bodies insubstan-
tial?) Slowly but surely Christian thinkers would ask
questions for which Scripture did not have an answer;
many would go on to create their own theories.

Irenaeus of Lyons, a contemporary of Tatian and a
native of Asia Minor living in Roman Gaul, was not an
original thinker but one who tried to organize Christian
belief, specifically for Greek-educated Christians who
had difficulty with some of the crudities of the Bible, especially the Old Testament. For Irenaeus, Satan was an
angel, created good since God can only create the good.
But then Irenaeus had to explain how Satan fell from
heaven; what sin did he commit? Irenaeus concluded
that Satan was envious of Adam, God's new creation,
and made in the divine image, unlike the angels. But
God did not make Adam until after he had created the
earth, so Satan fell from heaven only later than that.
Like other early Christians, Irenaeus could not escape
from the Jewish Watcher Angels who came down to
earth subsequent to the creation because they were
tempted by female bodies. Irenaeus had a low view of
Eve, so the ancient Jewish account would not have presented any difficulty with him. But for Irenaeus, there
was even more. When Satan fell because of his envy of

Adam, he did so alone. Only at the time of Noah did other angels end up with him.

Fearful of heresy, Irenaeus created a theological method that emphasized Scripture and the traditions of episcopal teaching, which he demonstrated had reached back to the apostles. He loathed heresy because the devil was behind it and, following Polycarp, he defined heresy as what a bishop condemned as heresy.

Further advancing the second-century wandering from Scripture, Irenaeus firmly asserted the link between Satan and the Antichrist.

Across the Mediterranean in Roman North Africa a priest named Tertullian created the first theology in the Latin language. Scholars call the African church a "gathered church," a church that deliberately cut itself off from the evil world around it and maintained a vigorous discipline to keep the world out. Tertullian so loathed the pagans and their culture and society that he believed that one of the *joys* of heaven would be watching the damned—mostly pagans—be incinerated in hell. Tertullian did not advance the theology of Satan; he accepted Irenaeus' view that Satan sinned by envy. But he did add a number of details that became part of the satanic tradition, such as his claim that Satan was not only an angel but the most important angel in heaven. This idea became very popular in later centuries because it explained Satan's envy that so lowly a creature as a human was created in the divine image.

Tertullian saw the devil almost everywhere, ranging from harmful weather to heresy. But he did add a dangerous note about heretics as well as pagans and Jews. People cannot be morally good if they do not have true beliefs; false belief makes a morally good life impossible. For him, every non-Christian was morally evil. As Russell put it, this "laid the basis for centuries of persecution of Jews, heretics, and witches" (*The Devil*, 99).

Tertullian prized what he defined as the Truth, and that caused him to denounce as untrue a variety of pagan practices such as idolatry, astrology, and magic. But he also opposed attending the theater on the grounds that actors *lied* when they played characters they were not. Going even further, he actually condemned the use of makeup and hair dye because this meant the woman was lying about her appearance. Naturally, Satan was behind all this.

Silly as this last example sounds, it became popular for preachers in the ancient and medieval worlds. Sermons survive that warn women that they will go to hell for using makeup, comparing a woman's plucking out an eyebrow to the demons painfully plucking her skin in hell. One of Tertullian's most famous sayings was one to women: "You are the devil's gateway." To be sure the Bible contains much misogynism from the Garden of Eden to the restrictions on women in early Christian liturgies, but this went beyond all. For centuries, some religious leaders would see women as inherently evil, threats to the virtue of men, and aligned to the devil.

By the third century the intellectual leadership of Christianity centered on Alexandria in Egypt. Much influenced by Greek thought, two great Alexandrians, Clement (ca. 150–ca. 220) and Origen (ca. 185–253) would bring philosophical notions and detailed scriptural exegesis to the question of the devil.

Clement correctly perceived that the real issue for Christians was not the devil but the problem of evil or theodicy. If God is all-good, and he can create only what is good, where does evil come from? Clement suggested that evil is nothing, literally *nothing* since it is the absence of the good—a theory known as the privation theory and used by many later theologians. But this theory had problems, particularly no Scriptural base. Indeed, Scripture sees evil in many circumstances and presents it as a potent and existing force in people's lives. Certainly the devil was an existing being for the early Christians. And, in the Lord's Prayer (Matt 6:23), did Jesus really ask his Father to deliver us from something nonexistent? And on the practical religious level, how does one deal with an absence? Yet Clement had added an important element to the discussion, a different, often higher level of thinking that went well beyond the unanalyzed repetition of biblical and apocryphal themes. Clement challenged other Christians to think seriously about the phenomenon of evil.

Clement's student Origen was the greatest biblical exegete of Christian antiquity. A genuine genius, he wanted to rid Christianity of what he considered nonsense. He studied the Bible relentlessly, including going to Jewish teachers to learn Hebrew, thus attaining a skill that very few ancient Christian scholars had. He also looked carefully at the literary devices in Scripture and labored endlessly to establish the correct text of the Bible, an astonishing achievement in an era when all books were copied by hand and mistakes were not only common but inevitable.

Origen believed that apocalyptic thinking simply made no sense since it included endless visions that often contradicted one another and that never came true in the real world. He quickly succeeded in marginalizing apocalypticism. After Origen, the book of Revelation was less and less perceived as a blueprint for the end, although elements of that book, such as Satan's being the Eden serpent, would survive. He guaranteed that no apocalyptic movement—and there were many—would ever dominate the church.

Origen's remarkable knowledge of the Bible convinced him of something else, too: some parts of the Bible do not make sense literally, historically, or morally. But the Bible contained God's truth, so if it does not make sense to us, then we have not understood it clearly and must delve further into the text. Early on, Origen turned to a literary device well known among Greeks, Romans, and diasporan Jews—namely, allegory.

Allegory is the literary theory that a text can be written on one level, but its true meaning exists on another level. For example, Origen could not accept the biblical notion of God the mass murderer. He wrote that when the Israelites destroyed the city of Jericho and killed all its inhabitants, including newborn infants, what that passage really meant was that the people of Jericho represented, *allegorically*, our sins. And the infants? We must extinguish even the smallest of our sins.

This method has obvious difficulties: if the text does not mean what it says literally, how is one to discover what the true allegorical meaning is? Origen realized that, but he saved the Old Testament for the Christians by showing them that they did not have to believe in a deity that many of them found difficult and occasionally revolting. Until the twelfth century allegory was the favored exegesis of Christian scholars.

Allegory also impacted the Christian view of the devil. The Old Testament makes many references to monsters, such as Leviathan in the book of Job. Origen did not believe in sea monsters nor in a God who would battle with them. How demeaning for the creator of heaven and earth to be punching it out with a sea serpent!

So what did these biblical monsters represent allegorically? Satan. God battles constantly with Satan, and the Bible represents God battling with monsters. What else can such passages possibly mean? This may seem forced to us, but we can appreciate how educated Christians would have been relieved to know that they did not have to believe in sea monsters. This type of allegory also increased the Old Testament references to Satan from a mere three to dozens.

Origen made two other great contributions to the Christian understanding of the devil.

As a biblical scholar, he resented the continuing influence of the Jewish apocryphal books on Christian thinking. Many Christians believed that Satan sinned his way out of heaven with his envy of Adam and Eve, which meant he sinned after the creation. Origen did not feel comfortable with that because it reeked of the Jewish Watcher Angels theory. But how to determine Satan's sin?

Brilliantly, this biblical scholar used the Bible. He accepted that the Eden serpent was Satan. What sin did he get Adam and Eve to commit? Disobedience, right? Actually, no. That was their second sin. Before their disobedience Satan promised them that they would be like gods—that is, *they would be more than they had a right to be*. In Greek, such a desire was called *húbris*, usually translated "pride" but meaning far more.

In the Greek myths, Phaethon, a man, drove the chariot of his father the sun god Helios, something no mortal should even hope to do. Phaethon could not control the sun chariot as it swerved and pitched. The raging, erratic course of the sun was endangering the world, so the gods struck Phaethon down. Another Greek mortal named Bellerophon decided to ride his flying horse Pegasus to the top of Mount Olympus, the home of the gods, where he had no right to be. The gods struck him down as well. Both are classic examples of *húbris*.

Besides Eden, this sin of *húbris* appears a second time in the opening chapters of Genesis because in chapter 11 the humans building the tower of Babel want its top to "reach into the heavens," where they have no right to go. God prevents this act of *húbris* by confusing their language.

Origen had his answer. Satan's sin was pride, wanting to be more than he had a right to be, wanting to be

like God, the same sin that he would first tempt Adam
and Eve to commit. Ever since Origen Christians have
accepted that Satan's sin was pride.

Origen also took an idea from his master Clement
and gave it a theological base. That was the salvation
of Satan. This sounds strange because most Christians
believe that Satan is so thoroughly evil that he is beyond
salvation. But Origen argued that to deny that God can
save Satan is to compromise the divine nature by denying the universality of God's salvific power. But Origen
lost on this one, and later generations of smaller minds
denounced him as a heretic for his views on this point.
But this idea demonstrates how later theologians were
taking questions about Satan well beyond the New
Testament.

Origen was persecuted for his faith by a pagan
Roman government, but in the early fourth century,
the Roman emperor Constantine (306–37) converted
to Christianity. Free from threats, the Christians evangelized on a vast scale, and by the late fourth century
most of the empire had become Christian.

An end to the persecutions! A dream come true. But
a number of Christians saw another side to this. They
idealized the church of the persecutions, seeing it as a
heroic period in which the Christians had more unity
and were even a morally better people. For these Christians, the martyrs who gave their lives for their faith
were the true heroes. But now that those heroes were
gone, who would replace them?

The monks.

In every society there have been people who felt the
need "to get away from it all," to leave the world and its
trappings and go off to live a simple life. The ancient
Greeks had philosophical communities; the Qumran
Jews considered Jerusalem a sort of ancient Las Vegas, a
"Sin City" to be avoided, and so they fled to the desert.

Even before the reign of Constantine there were Christians who went off to a wilderness to be alone with God, but their numbers increased significantly in the fourth century as a genuine monastic movement began, initially in Egypt but then spreading to other areas. But the Egyptian monks most influenced Christian views of the devil.

The Egyptian monks had traditional ascetic, self-denying views. They believed that by purifying their bodies through abstinence from sexual activity, comfortable homes, and tasty foods, they would improve themselves spiritually. They lived simply in desert huts, ate coarse food, and, as one Egyptian *abba* put it, they "fled women and bishops," by which he meant sexual temptation and what he considered to be the bishops' worldly status.

For the monks, the Egyptian desert represented a parched Garden of Eden, similar to the world God created before humans spoiled it. Visitors to the desert reported seeing monks who went about naked in imitation of Adam and Eve before the Fall.

Yet the desert also represented something far different from Eden. The desert was the place of Moses' exile and the place of the forty-year wanderings of the Exodus Hebrews. For Isaiah, one of the crimes of the king of Babylon was making the world a desert (14:17). For Jeremiah the prophet, the desert was "a land of drought and deep darkness" (2:6). But it could be even worse. The wild satyrs lived in the desert as did the fearsome she-demon Lilith. Most dangerously, the desert was the abode of Satan, as Jesus himself learned when Satan tempted him there. The monks were heading into very dangerous territory.

Although there were literally thousands of Egyptian monks, the greatest was the long-lived Saint Antony (251–356) whose "life" was written by the Alexandrian

bishop and theologian Athanasius (296–373). When
Christians wrote about saints, they practiced a discipline called *hagiography*, Greek for "writing about the
holy." The hagiographer included biographical information about the saint but focused much on the saint's
spiritual life. Today that would mean the saint's prayer
life, spiritual practices, and relation to God, but in the
ancient and medieval worlds it also included—usually
very heavily—the saint's miracles. In this tradition,
Athanasius's *Life of Saint Antony* emphasizes the saint's
miraculous powers, and understandably so since Antony
really needed them to fight off the devil.

The hagiography of Antony represented the first
Christian demonology, the first time any Christian
writer devoted a major book primarily to demonic activity.
Athanasius kept his focus on Antony but mostly on his
struggles with Satan.

Satan considered the desert to be his homeland, and
on one of the many occasions he appeared to Antony, he
claimed that the monks were turning the desert into a
city by civilizing it and making it a cosmos.

Satan repeatedly tried to drive Antony away, appearing to him in any number of guises, usually mon-
strous animals because for Athanasius, Satan was the
archetypal shape-shifter. Satan also used a variety of
temptations to get Antony to sin and thus to convince
him that his spiritual self-exile to the desert had failed.
Besides the familiar physical temptations, Satan tried
to make Antony feel guilty for having left his parentless
sister to go to the desert. When the devil did not suc-
ceed on his own, he sent hordes of other evil spirits to
attack and tempt Antony, all to no avail.

But if Satan could mask himself as an angel of light,
how could Antony be sure that the being appearing to
him was not actually an angel? Anthony practiced what
came to be called the "discernment of spirits," the prac-

tice of identifying good and evil ones. A simple man, Antony took a simple approach. If the spirit made him feel ill at ease and upset, it could not be a good one; if it made him feel calm and at peace, it must be a good one. Later Christians would develop this discipline.

This book also shows the impact of early thinking about the devil. In book 2 of *The Life of Saint Antony*, Athanasius wrote, "they [the demons] appear in shapes such as the Lord revealed the devil to Job," and then Athanasius repeated the description of the sea monster Leviathan in chapter 41 of the book of Job. Here Athanasius followed Origen's interpretation of the Old Testament monsters as symbols of the devil, which allowed the Christians to find far more than three references to Satan in the Old Testament.

Athanasius wrote the best-selling book of Greek Christian antiquity, an exciting tale of supernatural combat set in a wilderness, a ferocious opponent, a sturdy hero, and the eventual victory of the good. This book and others like it, such as the similar, best-selling Latin Christian book about a monk and devils, *The Life of Martin of Tours* by Sulpicius Severus in Gaul (ca. 400), forever changed the Christian view of the devil.

First, Athanasius made the devil a worthwhile subject of scholarly study. The Alexandrian bishop was one of the greatest theologians of the ancient church and one of the founders of Christian trinitarian theology. That such a scholar could devote himself to studying the works and pomps of the devil gave demonology a strong legitimacy.

Second, he supported some of the already existing theories, including that of his fellow Alexandrian Origen about allegorizing the Old Testament monsters.

Third, and most important, he gave the devil a powerful immediacy in the lives of all Christians. The faithful had always believed that Satan tempted people, but Athansius portrayed demonic temptation as relentless. The devil tempted Antony at every opportunity and even tried to create more opportunities for temptation. After *The Life of Saint Antony*, Christians viewed demonic temptation as a constant threat; every moment of every day Satan was looking for weaknesses to exploit to get us to sin. This was not a devil to discuss or theorize about; this was one to fear.

The desert monks left quite a legacy and often had more influence on the Christian view of the devil than the Bible and theologians.

Many other ancient theologians wrote about the devil, but just one more requires our attention as one who changed the Christian understanding of Satan: the North African bishop Augustine of Hippo (354–430).

Augustine was the greatest Latin theologian of the ancient church, and he influenced theology in myriad ways, but his most powerful influence on Christianity as a whole was his creation of original sin.

His creation? Yes, because original sin does not appear in Genesis or the letters of Paul or anywhere else in Scripture. In 393 Augustine put it into the Christian vocabulary and created a theology to go with it.

We know the basics: Adam and Eve lived sinless lives in the Garden of Eden until Satan tempted them to disobey God and commit what became known as original sin. But far more was involved than just the first sin. For Augustine, when Adam and Eve sinned, all of their descendants—that is, every one of us—would be born with the guilt of that sin, which can only be erased by Christian baptism. But even after baptism, original sin continues to impact us because Augustine believed that it weakened our wills in such a way that we cannot do anything good on our own but must rely upon God's freely-given grace. Into this demanding theology Augustine mixed predestination and divine foreknowledge.

This is a complicated, brilliant, almost intimidating theology that deserves detailed explication, but here we can only note that Augustine brought the Garden of Eden and thus Satan the tempter into the center of Christian theology. We sin because of what the devil tempted our primal parents to do. A minor episode barely mentioned in the Old Testament had now become one of the central elements of Christian teaching. The impact of original sin on Christian thinking guaranteed that Satan would have great importance in Christian theology and daily life, and his existence would go unquestioned for a millennium and a half.

These are the basic contributions of post–New Testament, early Christian writings about Satan. Later theologians, especially in the Medieval and Reformation periods, elaborated upon them but never essentially altered them. As we shall see in the next chapter, only in the nineteenth century did matters change. The rise of modern geology and evolutionary biology made the historicity of Genesis 1–11 impossible to accept, and thus Satan as the Eden serpent disappeared as did the Watcher Angels and the traditional understanding of original sin. The parallel rise of modern biblical exegesis demonstrated that the early Christians had borrowed and adapted many of their ideas about Satan from Jewish apocryphal works, some quite mythological in character and content. This exegesis also questioned the complete historicity of the gospels, demonstrated the different attitudes toward Satan in the New Testament, and relegated the book of Revelation to a set of confusing and conflicting visions of one particular writer. These two forces continue to impact the Christian understanding of Satan who now has to live in the modern world or, at best, in the biblical world as now understood by contemporary science and exegesis. Can he survive?

CHAPTER TEN

Satan Today

According to the Gallup organization, 92 percent of contemporary Americans believe in God, a figure that often astounds people in other technologically advanced countries (Frank Newport, "Americans More Likely to Believe in God Than Devil, 2007). But that figure must be parsed a bit. People may conclude that there is indeed a Supreme Being, but they may not be convinced that any religious group can adequately claim to carry that Being's message to humans. Having said that, we must note that most *theists*, those who believe in a deity, are also religious. Even those who are not religious usually still depend on religions for their view of God. For example, I know people who have left the Roman Catholic Church but whose view of God either matches or derives from what that church teaches.

Belief in the devil is also high, 68 percent, with another 20 percent saying they do not believe in the devil and 12 percent saying they are unsure. Modern polls, however, do not ask the type of question that was asked in 1970s—namely, whether the devil is an actual being or a symbol of an impersonal evil force. The percentage of believers in Satan also relates to education. The better educated people are, the less likely they are to believe in Satan, but the figure is still at 55 percent for those with postgraduate degrees (law, medicine, science). Furthermore, the more religious people are, the more likely they are to believe; the less religious they are, the less likely they are to believe.

Yet at the end of the twentieth century, the National Academy of Sciences reported that 72 percent of scientists do not believe in God, although the numbers vary a bit with disciplines. Another 20 percent of scientists were not sure whether God existed (Larson and Witham, 1998). Given the role that scientists play in modern civilizations, this is a troubling statistic for religious people. But if the overall numbers of belief in the devil are impressive for people in an educated, science-oriented, information-driven society, they are much lower than the numbers in previous generations where belief in Satan approached 100 percent.

To these figures one can add some practical questions about belief in Satan today. If someone were arrested for a crime and pleaded "not guilty" on the grounds that the devil had irresistibly tempted him to commit the crime ("the devil made me do it"), would those who believe in the devil find that an adequate excuse? To push this a bit, if a person who believed in the devil was the victim of that crime, would she or he accept such an answer? If no, why not? Sociologists of religion have repeatedly observed that many people who claim to believe in Satan are reluctant to specify any particular sinful act that was prompted by him rather than by such human desires as greed or lust.

When people tell relatives or friends that the devil has been appearing to them and torturing them, would those friends or relatives who believe in the devil recommend that these people seek out a minister, an exorcist, or a psychiatrist? And to return to the beginning of this book, why are believers not enraged that sports teams carry the devil's name? And how can they attend events at which the fearsome enemy of God and humanity is represented by someone in a silly costume trying to get the fans to cheer?

We must recall that belief in Satan is like belief in God—a matter of faith. If God's existence could be proven, there would be no atheists; if it could be disproven, there would be no theists. No one can prove that Satan exists nor can anyone prove that he does not exist. What can be proven is that over the centuries belief in Satan has diminished. Here is a brief survey of how many Christians moved from a firm belief in Satan to a questioning attitude or even to disbelief.

As we just saw, the early Christians, those of the first five centuries, put together the basic teaching on Satan, although the further they went from the New Testament period, the more willing they were to go beyond biblical teaching.

The medieval Christians did not really advance the theology of the devil so much as increase his presence in church and society. The first visual portrayal of Satan is part of a mosaic in a sixth-century church in Ravenna, Italy. A flood of illustrations would follow, often depicting Satan like the Greek deity Pan with cloven hooves, shaggy body, and horns.

The devil also played a great role in popular literature. Medieval hagiographies portray the saints repelling Satan over and over again. This type of literature would appeal to peasants and illiterate townspeople routinely bullied and abused by powerful nobles who were usually exempt from responsibility—much less punishment—for any harm they had done or abuses they had committed. How good to see the ultimate bully and abuser be routed by the saint!

The devil also played a great role in sermon literature of the Middle Ages as preachers tried to get the people to lead good lives and found that fear of Satan and hell often had more impact than pleas to do what is right. Belief in Satan also reached into the highest realms of medieval literature as the great Italian poet Dante (1265–1321) proved in his *Divine Comedy* and especially in the first segment, *Inferno*.

A holdover from the ancient Christians also poisoned the Middle Ages as "enemies" of the church were believed to be in league with Satan. Throughout the period these enemies included Jews, Muslims, pagans, and heretics. Later in the Middle Ages people saw Satan in league with witches, who were mostly women. Sometimes the beliefs bordered on the ridiculous as people saw the devil behind thunderstorms, poor harvests, and, for one theologian, a fly whose buzzing about distracted him from writing a book.

The Reformation of the sixteenth century made the problem even worse as Catholics and Protestants routinely accused one another of being in league with Satan. In that same century, but even more so in the next one, European Christians believed that Satan had launched a war against them by employing witches. For more than a century, hundreds of thousands of innocent people, mainly women, were arrested a tried as witches. The number of those executed is unknown, but it exceeded one hundred thousand. Never had the devil seemed more powerful.

Belief in the devil was strong and secure, but scientists would change that. In the sixteenth and seventeenth centuries, scholars such as Nicholas Copernicus, Johannes Kepler, Galileo Galilei, and Isaac Newton created a new understanding of the cosmos, and they did so by reason alone, not challenging but simply working without the Bible or ecclesiastical authority and teaching. Although this cosmological revolution is best known, other scientists did extensive work in optics and on the circulation of the blood, and they too did so without reference to Christian beliefs. Faith remained strong, but people increasingly came to rely upon reason rather than faith to answer questions, not least because scientists had to prove what they said rather than ask (or command) people to believe. Inevitably scientific findings began to impact religious belief. To give but one example, comets were widely believed to be signs of impending disaster coming from God, but scientists proved that they were just physical objects moving through space.

Soon scholars began to apply reason and scientific thinking extensively to matters of faith, although we will deal only with evil. Seventeenth- and eighteenth-century intellectuals asked why God allowed evil. Why did not God just restrain or even destroy Satan? Why did God condemn the entire human race to eternal damnation because two prehistoric people took a bite out of a piece of fruit? Why did not a merciful God just forgive Adam and Eve?

The challenge to traditional views of Satan and evil came to a head in the nineteenth century. As we have seen, original sin played an enormous role in Christian theology, and it depended on the actual existence of Adam and Eve, the Garden, and the eating of the fruit. But original sin depended on far more than that.

The Garden of Eden account is an integral part of the larger narrative in Genesis, chapters 1–11, and it cannot be separated from the other accounts that include a six-day creation, extensive lifespans of some ancient people like Methuselah, the Noachic Flood, and the tower of Babel. Furthermore, a literal understanding of Genesis 1–11 also provided enough information for biblical scholars to determine how old the world is, and, in the seventeenth century Anglican bishop James Ussher concluded that the creation occurred in 4,004 BC, a date widely accepted by religious scholars of that era.

In the nineteenth century, formidable challenges to the literal interpretation of Genesis 1–11 began when scientific geology demonstrated that the world is much older than six thousand years and that there was no geological evidence for a worldwide flood. Also in that century, evolutionary biology demonstrated that animals were not created by God in a few days but rather evolved over millions of years.

Scientists, who set out to practice science and not to challenge biblical truth, had made it impossible for educated people to accept the historicity of the Genesis creation account. Many religious people accepted these findings and set out to rethink Genesis and original sin, but most Christians hoped to keep the traditional views.

But to their dismay, modern biblical scholarship likewise challenged the literal character of Genesis 1–11. Exegetes insisted upon examining the Bible in its historical setting, and they recognized that ancient people simply did not view the world and God as we do. The new exegetes also examined literary devices in the Bible, and they concluded that ancient peoples were comfortable using myths and thus did not always produce accounts meant to be taken literally. The new exegetes particularly focused on the opening chapters of Genesis.

It is difficult if not impossible for us to realize the impact these new movements had upon believers and the challenge they presented to much traditional teaching. If Adam and Eve did not exist, then neither did the tree or the diabolic serpent, and original sin as customarily understood had to be rethought. We are just not born evil because we inherited the stain of sin from a primeval couple who never existed. Furthermore, these new exegetes refused to accept Jewish apocryphal notions, such as an angelic revolt, as biblical.

Some traditionalist Christian leaders dealt with challenge by rejecting the new ideas. Between 1913 and 1917, conservative Protestant scholars produced a series of books called *The Fundamentals* to challenge the new exegesis. These books proved to be immensely popular with conservative pastors, and eventually the people who relied upon *The Fundamentals* acquired the name fundamentalists. But despite these reactionary efforts, the new exegesis eventually came to dominate leading universities in Great Britain, Canada, and the United States, as well Catholic and mainline Protestant seminaries, even though it challenged many of the traditional notions about the Bible and thus about Satan. (This exegesis has been used throughout this book.)

Then more challenges to the traditional ideas about evil appeared. By the end of the nineteenth century and the beginning of the twentieth, three new disciplines to study human behavior made their appearance: anthropology, sociology, and psychology. All three would change our view of evil and, inevitably, of Satan.

Anthropologists studied many cultures, particularly primitive ones, and they showed how notions of right and wrong would change from culture to culture. Modern Western societies consider people to have an inviolable right to life, but anthropologists found far northern cultures in which a common practice was for leaders to kill people thought to be too weak to survive the impending winter so that the tribe would not "waste" some of the precious winter food supply. A less violent example of different cultural views would be the peoples of equatorial Africa, South America, and the Pacific, who go about with most of their bodies uncovered, a practice that would be considered sinful in most other places. Anthropologists showed that notions of evil can vary from culture to culture, and thus what one group considers evil and thus inspired by Satan is in reality a manifestation of different cultural values and environment.

Sociologists demonstrated the extent to which our behavior is determined by our social groupings. Boys in poor, rough neighborhoods where "socializing" involves joining a gang will often have a very different view of right and wrong from boys growing up in stable, financially comfortable neighborhoods where socializing means joining the school swim team. Obviously some boys from the "worse" neighborhoods grow up to become model citizens while some boys from "better" neighborhoods become criminals, but sociologists have conclusively shown that social groupings impact our views of many things, including right and wrong. Sinful behavior can result from social situations and not just from demonic temptation.

Psychology demonstrated the impact that family upbringing and personal interactions have upon our notions of right and wrong. The most striking example of this involves parental and spousal abuse. Two-thirds of all male abusers were themselves abused as children. Growing up in such circumstances severely weakened their abilities to deal with problems in a nonviolent way. On more general issues, psychology demonstrated that the desires for money, sex, and power—usually thought by Christians to be consequences of original sin—are absolutely normal, although modes of fulfilling those normal desires can be morally wrong. For example, there is nothing wrong with desiring money, but there is something very wrong with stealing it to satisfy that desire.

Psychology also forced people to rethink something that had been common in Christian history, such as dreams and visions of evil spirits. In 1692 in Salem Village, Massachusetts Bay Colony, people were executed as witches because several adolescent girls claimed that these "witches" had appeared to them, either in dreams or visions. Today when people claim to have demonic apparitions, family members and friends would more likely urge them to seek psychiatric care rather than accept their views that these disturbances are demonic. The same would be true for those claiming to be possessed. (It must be noted that when people claim to be possessed, the most skeptical responses usually come from church authorities.)

So common is psychology in understanding what had previously been accepted as behavior caused by demonic temptation that seminaries include psychology in their curricula for priests and ministers.

We have come a long way from the first century when the earliest Christians were using the Old Testament and the Jewish apocrypha along with the teachings of Jesus and his disciples to understand who Satan is and what he does. None of those first Christians could have envisioned a world in which leading intellectuals, such as physical scientists, would not even believe in God, much less the devil. Nor could they have comprehended how people would not see demonic temptation behind someone's sinful acts but would instead want to know the "sinner's" personal and social background. And, of course, people who took the devil so seriously could never have understood how people could name things after him or even make jokes about him.

Does this mean that Satan does not exist and that belief about him is basically a relic of an earlier age? Not at all. But it does mean that Christians must take a serious look at their traditional teachings about Satan.

To many people, reconsidering traditional teachings is a thinly disguised excuse to "modernize" those teachings just to appease contemporary critics. If Christians have believed something for twenty centuries, why change it now?

One reason would be that there are very few things that Christians have believed for twenty centuries. Earlier on we saw how the post–New Testament Christians created the word "trinity" as a means to establish the unity of God and the independence and equality of the Father, Son, and Holy Spirit. When fourth-century bishops at the Council of Nicea proclaimed the doctrine of the Trinity and used some Greek philosophical terminology to explain it, contemporary, "traditional" Christians accused the bishops of "modernizing" belief. Now, of course, Nicea has become tradition.

Other examples abound. Many Christian churches have sacraments, but the word "sacrament" does not appear in the New Testament. Most Roman Catholics would be surprised to learn that the word "pope" does not appear in the New Testament. Virtually every "traditional" element in Christianity was an innovation at some point—and was usually denounced as such.

To look at this issue a bit differently, if people really want to go back to the beginning, look what we become stuck with: a God who kills everyone in the world except the eight people on the ark; a creation story that defies the findings of modern science; and obviously mythical tales such as a man being swallowed by a sea creature and vomited out three days later. This is what Russell meant by the genetic fallacy, ossifying as binding truth beliefs and practices that later, sincere believers do not and cannot accept.

Over the centuries most Christians have come to recognize that not everything attached to their faith had the same status and that some things could change and develop. The ancients believed in God and we believe in God, but we do not believe that God drops down to the field of battle to slug it out with the pagans (Deut 20:4). We believe in a blessed afterlife, but we do not believe that heaven is above the sky.

Doubters might concede these points, but surely our understanding of Jesus has not changed or developed, right?

To demonstrate that the understanding of Jesus has changed and developed, we have no need to compare the ancient with the modern. Instead we can compare the ancient with the ancient. The Christology of Mark's gospel differs considerably from the Christology of John's. Mark speaks of Jesus as the Son of God in a unique way, not just as all humans are the daughters and sons of God; nevertheless Mark's gospel does not identify Jesus as divine while John's gospel does so twice (1:1; 20:28) and portrays Jesus as the incarnate divine Word. Christian understanding of Jesus had developed in the decades between the writing of Mark and the writing of John. Postbiblical advances in doctrine often continued what can be found in Scripture itself.

So if Scripture can allow for development in the Christian understanding of Jesus, there can be nothing wrong when modern Christians want to rethink what they actually believe about Satan.

Surveys show that many contemporary Christians do not even believe that the devil exists, and so that would be a good place to start. Can Satan exist?

If we believe that God created us, there is no reason to think that he did not create any other types of creatures. (It would be depressing to think that we are the best that God can do.) In a universe of two hundred billion galaxies (based on current estimations), it is almost unthinkable that no other planet has intelligent life and, if so, those beings would be different from us yet still be divine creations.

There is, thus, no reason to believe that God could not or did not create creatures other than us, creatures that function in this world and who are less physical than we are or possibly even not physical at all. There is also no reason why such creatures could not have intelligence and will and could interact with one another and with us in ways that we do not realize or recognize. Like us, some of them could use their will to disobey God and to do evil, and, like too many humans, they might choose to spread their evil to others. In sum, there could well be evil spirits who wish to do evil to other beings; Satan *could* exist.

The problem is how we understand Satan.

Before going on to that, let me put in a personal note. As a lifelong Christian, I believe that religion can be a very positive force in life. Churches, Protestant, Orthodox, and Catholic, open soup kitchens, provide refuges for the poor, and run inexpensive clothing shops, all maintained by people serving their Lord. Churches also firmly oppose our society's rampant consumerism, the attitude that people be evaluated by what they have, not by who they are—an attitude that completely devalues the poor, who were so special to Jesus. Churches have also been on the front lines in combating such vile practices as human trafficking—a horror that governments have done little to stop or prevent.

So churches have good values, but what has all this to do with whether or not people believe in Satan?

When churches ask believers to believe nonsense, they turn those people off and run the risk that when they speak of something important, such as justice for the poor, people will not listen. When church leaders tell believers that they must accept, contrary to all modern science, that the world is only six thousand years old, do those leaders really believe that people will listen when they tell them that consumerism is an evil that hurts the impoverished?

Evil is real, it is dangerous, and it must be taken seriously. But it will not be taken seriously if church leaders tell people that in order to combat evil, they must believe in ancient Jewish myths about angels who were lured from heaven by earth women using makeup. It is time to move beyond the traditional image of Satan. I cannot claim to know exactly how this might be done, but here are some suggestions.

1. We must acknowledge the harm that a simplistic belief in Satan has done in the past, from executing witches to imaging Jews as devils to justifying the destruction of supposedly devil-worshipping Native Americans by the invading Christian Europeans. This is part of our history just as much as those parts we like to cite, such as the heroic deaths of the martyrs and the great works of charity. Seeing demonic influence or at least claiming to do so has enabled Christians for centuries to legitimize vile and violent actions. We must be extremely cautious in claiming that some act or some person has been motivated by Satan.

2. We must avoid allowing belief in Satan to excuse us from responsibility for what we do. Satan does not make us do it, and no church has ever taught that. Churches teach that Satan tempts us, but we either withstand it or give in to the temptation. We do evil on our own, and Satan cannot be used to exculpate us.

3. Churches must abandon any trace of the Halloween/ Hollywood aspects of Satan: the arched eyebrows, the pointed ears and beard, the furry body, the cloven hoofs, and anything else that fosters a mythic and thus unreal image of a being whom churches want people to take seriously.

4. On a more elevated level, we must take theodicy seriously. The fundamental problem for believers

is not that Satan goes about the world seeking the ruin of souls but that God allows him to do so. Scholars who do theodicy do not worry about Satan, not because they do not necessarily believe in him, but because they know this is the real problem: if Satan does not exist, then God permits evil; if Satan does exist, then God permits him to do evil. The question always boils down to God and evil, and no discussion of Satan can be understood separately from theodicy.

5. We must accept the findings of modern science, especially disciplines such as anthropology, sociology, and psychology, which examine the motives people have for what they do. When I was a freshman at Boston College, the Jesuit Scripture professor gave the students a good maxim for approaching the Bible: *miracula non multiplicanda sunt*—"Miracles are not to be multiplied." By that he meant we should look for human and natural explanations to difficult biblical passages and not to throw in the supernatural every time we encounter a problem. The same applies here: we should not look for supernatural explanations for evil acts when scientific findings or just common sense can provide human or natural explanations.

6. We must accept the findings of modern biblical scholarship and abandon notions that no contemporary, mainline Christian scholar takes seriously. There never was a rebellion in heaven. There never was a Garden of Eden. There never was a talking serpent. Holding on to these notions because Christians living before the rise of modern exegesis did makes no sense. We no longer accept traditional biblical ideas about slavery, about the second-class status of women, about a geocentric cosmos, and so

many other elements we know to be factually wrong or unacceptable to modern Christians. Biblical scholars are not the enemies of the faith. They are believers who are trying to make sense of the Bible for contemporary believers. We should be grateful for their work, and we should use it.

But how should we use modern exegesis when speaking of Satan? By citing the biblical belief in other-than-human creatures who actually exist and who may impact our lives and then see what the biblical accounts can tell us about such creatures.

If this seems a bit much to ask, recall that modern scholars who do not accept the historicity of the Garden of Eden still value the Genesis account as telling us that there is a gap between us and God, and that we are responsible for it. Some theologians would even argue that this gap exists before we were born as a part of human nature, thus preserving the biblical notion of evil continuing through generations. The Genesis account also shows God using "tough love" in expelling Adam and Eve from Eden but also caring for them, working through their descendant Abraham and then his descendants and, for Christians, working through Jesus Christ, whose descent the evangelist Luke traces back to Adam (Luke 3:38). Understanding the Eden account in this way has permitted theologians to preserve original sin but in a way compatible with modern exegesis.

This is what we must do with Satan: use contemporary exegetical methods to examine the biblical material for what it says about an evil spiritual being, and then try to see if that material can be given an interpretation that accords with or at least does not violate all that we know of evil from many disciplines and that accords with the teachings of the churches.

So, if it is still possible to speak of Satan today, can we ever say that a particular evil act resulted from satanic temptation rather than just an excess of greed or anger or lust? First we must recall that Satan's existence cannot be *proven*, and this in turn means that we cannot say that a particular sin can be proven to have been incited by him.

But when we acknowledge that accepting his existence is a matter of *faith*, we can ask if there are circumstances under which we might reasonably *believe* that Satan tempted us to a particular sinful act. Our best guide for making such a judgment is Scripture.

Theoretically Satan can provoke people to any evil act, but the New Testament mostly portrays him as trying to tempt Christians away from their fidelity to the church and also as possessing them in hope of destroying in them the image of God. We define ourselves in a variety of ways, such as age, gender, citizenship, and profession, but as believers we see the ultimate definition of our humanity as children of God, made in God's image and likeness, a definition we share with the Incarnate Son of God.

The forces that usually cause us to sin have no personality; they are inclinations which can be carried to evil lengths. Satan, on the other hand, does have a personality and thus a personal desire to see us fall into evil. Thus we can reasonably attribute an act to satanic influence when we engage in an evil so serious that it causes us to drift away from the church or to obscure, at least temporarily, the image of God within us.

Bibliography

Primary Sources

A modern translation and edition of the Bible. This book used *The New Revised Standard Version.* Division of Christian Education of the National Council of the Churches of Christ in the United States of America, 1989.

Sparks, H.D.F., ed. *The Apocryphal Old Testament*. Oxford: Clarendon Press, 1984.

Staniforth, Maxwell, trans. *Early Christian Writings*. London: Penguin Books, 1987.

Wise, Michael, et al., eds. *Dead Sea Scrolls: A New Translation*. San Francisco: Harper San Francisco, 1996.

Secondary Sources

Angel, Andy. *Angels: Ancient Whispers of Another World.* Eugene, OR: Cascade Books, 2012.

Bernstein, Alan E. *The Formation of Hell*. Ithaca, NY: Cornell University Press, 1993.

Britton, Davis. *Historical Dictionary of Mormonism*. Lanham, MA: Scarecrow Press, 2000.

Boureau, Alain. *Satan the Heretic*. Chicago: University of Chicago Press, 2006.

Brown, Raymond, et al., eds. *The Jerome Biblical Commentary*. Englewood Cliff, NJ: Prentice Hall, 1968; 2nd edition, 1999.

Catholic Answers. "Does the Catholic Church Believe in the Devil?" (*Catholic Answers*, 2013). Available at http://www.catholic.com/quickquestions/does-the-catholic-church-believe-in-the-devil.

Christ-Centered Mall. "Satan." (*Christ-Centered Mall*, 2012).
   Available at http://christcenteredmall.com/teachings
   /satan_3.htm.
De La Torre, Miguel, and Albert Hernandez. *The Quest of the
   Historical Satan*. Minneapolis: Fortress Press, 2011.
Delbanco, Andrew. *The Death of Satan*. New York: Farrar,
   Straus and Giroux, 1995.
Floyd, W. E. G. *Clement of Alexandria's Treatment of the
   Problem of Evil*. London: Oxford University Press, 1977.
Forsyth, Neil. *The Old Enemy: Satan and the Combat Myth*.
   Princeton, NJ: Princeton University Press, 1987.
Fuller, Robert. *Naming the Antichrist*. New York: Oxford Uni-
   versity Press, 1995.
Gregg, Joan. *Devils, Women, and Jews: Reflection on the
   Other in Medieval Sermon Stories*. Albany: State Univer-
   sity of New York Press, 1977.
Kelly, Henry Ansgar. *The Devil at Baptism: Ritual, Theology,
   and Drama*. Ithaca, NY: Cornell University Press, 1985.
———. *The Devil, Demonology, and Witchcraft: The Devel-
   opment of Christian Beliefs in Evil Spirits*. Eugene, OR:
   Wipf and Stock, 1974.
———. *Satan: A Biography*. New York: Cambridge Uni-
   versity Press, 2006. Best detailed study of Satan in early
   Christianity.
Larson, Edward J., and Larry Witham. "Leading Scientists
   Still Reject God." *Nature* 394. (July 23, 1998).
McGinn, Bernard. *Antichrist: Two Thousand Years of the
   Human Fascination with Evil*. San Francisco: HarperSan-
   Francisco, 1994.
Millikin, Jimmy. *Christian Doctrine for Everyman: An Intro-
   duction to Baptist Beliefs*. Bloomington, IN: Crossbooks
   Publishing, 2010.
Moriarty, Fredrick. "Isaiah 1–39." *Jerome Biblical Commen-
   tary*. Edited by Raymond E. Brown and Roland E. Murphy.
   Englewood Cliffs, NJ: Prentice-Hall, 1968.
Muchembled, Robert. *A History of the Bible*. Cambridge:
   Polity, 2003.
Newport, Frank. "Americans More Likely to Believe in God
   Than the Devil, Heaven More Than Hell." *Gallup*. (June

13, 2007). Available at http://www.gallup.com/poll/27877
/Americans-More-Likely-Believe-God-Than-Devil-Heaven
-More-Than-Hell.aspx.

Nowell, Irene. *101 Questions and Answers on Angels and
Devils*. Mahwah, NJ: Paulist Press, 2011.

Pagels, Elaine. *The Origins of Satan*. New York: Vintage
Books, 1996.

Patella, Michael. *Angels and Demons: A Christian Primer
of the Spiritual World*. Collegeville, MN: Liturgical Press,
2010.

Rorty, Amélie, ed. *The Many Faces of Evil: Historical Perspec-
tives*. New York: Routledge, 2001.

Russell, Jeffrey Burton. *The Devil: Perceptions of Evil from
Antiquity to Primitive Christianity*. Ithaca, NY: Cornell
University Press, 1977.

———. *Lucifer: The Devil in the Middle Ages*. Ithaca, NY:
Cornell University Press, 1984.

———. *Mephistopheles: The Devil in the Modern World*.
Ithaca, NY: Cornell University Press, 1986.

———. *Satan: The Early Christian Tradition*. Ithaca, NY:
Cornell University Press, 1981.

Van der Toon, Karl, et al., eds. *Dictionary of Deities and
Demons in the Bible*. 2nd edition. Grand Rapids, MI:
Eerdmans, 1999.